AEROSPACE BUSINESS LAW

AEROSPACE BUSINESS LAW

George V. d'Angelo

Q

QUORUM BOOKS
Westport, Connecticut • London

Library of Congress Cataloging-in-Publication Data

d'Angelo, George V.
Aerospace business law / George V. d'Angelo.
p. cm.
Includes bibliographical references and index.
ISBN 0–89930–892–9 (alk. paper)
1. Space industrialization—Law and legislation—United States.
2. Space industrialization—Law and legislation. I. Title.
KF2479.D36 1994
343.7309'79—dc20
[347.303974] 93–42764

British Library Cataloguing in Publication Data is available.

Library of Congress Catalog Card Number: 93–42764
ISBN: 0–89930–892–9

First published in 1994

Quorum Books, 88 Post Road West, Westport, CT 06881
An imprint of Greenwood Publishing Group, Inc.

Printed in the United States of America

The paper used in this book complies with the Permanent Paper Standard issued by the National Information Standards Organization (Z39.48–1984).

10 9 8 7 6 5 4 3 2 1

Contents

Abbreviations

AAU	Associated Aviation Underwriters
AECA	*Arms Export Control Act*
AFFARS	Air Force Supplement to the *Federal Acquisition Regulation*
AMSC	American Mobile Satellite Corporation
AMSS	aeronautical mobile satellite services
ARABSAT	Arab Satellite Communication Organization
ASPR	*Armed Services Procurement Regulation*
ASTRA	Application of Space Techniques Relating to Aviation (Panel)
ASTT	Advisory Service on Transfer and Development of Technology
ATA	Air Transport Administration
AT&T	American Telephone and Telegraph
BAFO	Best and Final Offer
BMDO	Ballistic Missile Defense Organization
BNSC	British National Space Centre
BT	British Telecommunications
CADIB	Centre Africain de Documentation et d'Information en matière de Brevets
CEPT	European Conference of Postal and Telecommunications Administration

CNES	Centre National d'Études Spatiales
COCOM	Coordinating Committee on Multilateral Export Controls
COFACE	Compagnie Française d'Assurance pour le Commerce Extérieur
COMSAT	Communication Satellite Corporation
COPUOS	Committee on the Peaceful Uses of Outer Space
CRDAs	cooperative research and development agreements
DAR	*Defense Acquisition Regulation*
DARA	Deutsche Agentur Für Raumfahrtagelegenheitgen
DARC	Defense Acquisition Regulatory Council
DARS	Defense Acquisition Regulatory System
DBS	direct broadcast satellite
DESD	Department of Economic and Social Development
DFARS	*DoD FAR Supplement*
DLR	German Aerospace Research Establishment
DMA	Defense Mapping Agency
DoD	Department of Defense
DoN	Department of the Navy
DOS	Department of Space
DOT	Department of Transportation
EC	European Community
ECA	Economic Commission for Africa
ECOSOC	Economic and Social Council
ECU	European currency unit
EEC	European Economic Community
ELDO	European Launcher Development Organisation
ELVs	expendable launch vehicles
ESA	European Space Agency
ESAPDIC	Patent Documentation and Information Center for English Speaking Africa
ESARIPO	African Regional Industrial Property Organization for English Speaking Office

ESCAP	Economic and Social Commission for Asia and the Pacific
ESRO	European Space Research Organisation
EU	European Union
EUMETSAT	European Organization for the Exploitation of Meteorological Satellites
EUTELSAT	European Telecommunications Satellite Organization
FAA	Federal Aviation Administration
FAO	Food and Agriculture Organization
FAR	*Federal Acquisition Regulations*
FCC	Federal Communications Commission
FDA	Food and Drug Administration
FTTA	*Federal Technology Transfer Act*
GATT	*General Agreement on Tariffs and Trade*
GSA	General Services Administration
GSFC	Goddard Space Flight Center
GTE	General Telephone and Electric
HBO	Home Box Office
IBRD	International Bank for Reconstruction and Development
ICAO	International Civil Aviation Organization
IFAD	International Fund for Agricultural Development
IMO	International Maritime Organization
INMARSAT	International Maritime Satellite Organization
INTELSAT	International Telecommunications Satellite Organization
INTERSPUTNIK	International Organization of Space Communications
IPC	International Patent Classification
ITA	International Trade Administration
ITAR	*International Traffic in Arms Regulation*
ITC	International Trade Commission (U.S.)
ITU	International Telecommunications Union

JFTC	Japanese Fair Trade Commission
kbps	kilobits per second
LEO	low-earth orbiting
LMSS	land mobile satellite service
MFARS	*Mapping Agency Federal Acquisition Regulation*
MMSS	maritime mobile satellite service
MSS	mobile satellite service
MTCR	*Missile Technology Control Regime*
NAPS	*Navy Acquisition Procedures Supplement*
NASA	National Aeronautics and Space Administration
NASDA	National Space Agency of Japan
NCRA	*National Cooperative Research Act*
NIST	National Institute of Standards and Technology
NOAA	National Oceanic and Atmospheric Administration
NSA	National Security Agency
NTIA	National Telecommunications Information Administration
NTTC	National Technology Transfer Center
OAPI	African Intellectual Property Organization
OCST	Office of Commercial Space Transportation
OEA	Office of Export Administration
OET	Office of Engineering and Technology
OFTEL	Office of Telecommunication
OMC	Office of Munitions Control
ORTAs	Offices of Research and Technology Applications
OSF	Office of Space Flight
PARTS	price analysis and review technique for spares/support equipment
PLF	partial loss factor
PSTN	public switched telephone network
RARC	Regional Administrative Radio Conferences
RBC	Request for Business Clearance
R&D	research and development

RDLP	research and development limited partnership
RDSS	radio determination satellite service
RFP	Request for Proposal
RTTC	Regional Technology Transfer Centers
SBIR	Small Business Innovation Research
SDIOS	Strategic Defense Initiative Organization
SOW	Statement of Work
TAIS	Technology Applications Information System
TRT	*Trademark Registration Treaty*
TT&C	tracking, telemetry, and command
UCC	*Uniform Commercial Code*
UHF	ultra-high frequency
UN	United Nations
UNCITRAL	United Nations Commission on International Trade Law
UNCSTD	United Nations Conference on Science and Technology for Development
UNCTAD	United Nations Conference on Trade and Development
UNDP	United Nations Development Program
UNDRO	Office of the United Nations Disaster Relief Coordinator
UNEP	United Nations Environment Program
UNESCO	United Nations Educational, Scientific, and Cultural Organization
UNIDO	United Nations Industrial Development Organization
USAU	United States Aviation Underwriters
USTR	United States Trade Representative
VSAT	very small aperture terminal
WARC	World Administrative Radio Conference
WIPO	World Intellectual Property Organization
WMO	World Meteorological Organization

Introduction

The need for this book became apparent to me in 1990. I had not been actively involved in the space business for a number of years and was trying to update my knowledge on the legal issues posed by the commercial development of space. I needed a general description of the various areas of space law from both a practitioner's and business person's perspective. I only found, however, in-depth studies of specific topics and some general, academic books on space law that, although well written, did not address my practical needs. I therefore had to spend considerable time researching the field. Realizing that many lawyers and business people who deal with this specialized and fast changing area have a similar need, I decided to make my study available to others, thus filling the gap in space business law publications.

The aim of this book is not to provide an in-depth analysis of specific areas. Policy discussion is also kept to a minimum, just enough to explain the context of certain laws and regulations. My basic goal is to bring together some of the legal issues presented by aerospace activities in order to provide a general but thorough picture of the overall framework of space commerce. Where the answers to specific problems are not provided, I will have achieved my goal if I can offer the reader an understanding of what the questions are.

Aerospace activities tend to be international in the sense that they involve governments and firms from many different countries. The United States, however, still leads the rest of the world in the development of space commerce in both scientific and economic terms. For that reason, greater emphasis is given to the regulations and procedures governing the industry in the United States and the perspective of this book is therefore an American one.

AEROSPACE BUSINESS LAW

Chapter One

The General Framework

Commercial space is a highly specialized and complex field that is difficult to appreciate without some knowledge of the entities involved and the main laws and regulations that govern it. For the benefit of the reader who is not already a specialist in the field, before exploring the various areas in detail, a general overview is given of the topics covered by this book. Following is a brief description of the main national and international governmental organizations that deal with aerospace activities and some of the applicable laws.

ENTITIES INVOLVED IN AEROSPACE ACTIVITIES

The Private Sector

When the words *aerospace industry* are mentioned, the names of a few giants come to mind automatically, such as McDonnell Douglas, Lockheed, TRW Inc., Martin Marietta, Hughes Aircraft Co., Rockwell International Corp., and General Dynamics. Other names are also starting to become familiar, including Deutche Aerospace, Aerospatiale, Alenia Spazio, British Aerospace, and many others. In fact, although the aerospace field is dominated by a few major firms that have grown over the years as contractors of the U.S. military, there are many small companies that manufacture components of large systems and are doing quite well. The transfer of technology from defense projects to civilian use is also creating many opportunities. As discussed in the chapter on technology transfer, both the National Aeronautics and Space Administration (NASA) and the Department of Defense have programs designed to encourage the use of these newly available technologies by small companies. This, of course, is in addition to the many provisions of the federal regulations regarding small and disadvantaged businesses.

International Organizations

The United Nations.[1] The United Nations (UN) has been active in outer space activities for over three decades through its own organs and departments and through specialized agencies. The main divisions of the United Nations proper that deal with space activities are listed below.

—Committee on the Peaceful Uses of Outer Space (COPUOS). It was established by the General Assembly in 1959. It has two standing subcommittees: the Scientific and Technical Subcommittee and the Legal Subcommittee. The committee provides an essential forum for guiding and coordinating the increasingly wide range of space activities handled by various divisions throughout the United Nations system.

—Outer Space Affairs Division. It is part of the Department of Political and Security Council Affairs. It implements the decisions of the General Assembly and of the Committee on the Peaceful Uses of Outer Space. It includes two sections: the Space Applications Section, which organizes and carries out the United Nations Program on Space Applications, and the Committee Services, Reports, and Research Section, which provides Secretariat services to the Committee, its Scientific and Technical Subcommittee, and its subsidiary technical bodies. The division also assists the secretariat of the Special Political Committee of the General Assembly during its consideration of outer space items.

—Department for Economic and Social Development (DESD). The department is in charge of a broad range of activities in the fields of cartography (surveying, mapping, and charting) geology, energy and mining, sea, and water resources. In the past, the department has been mostly interested in the application of satellite technology for geodesy, mapping, and earth resource surveys. More recently, cooperative activities of DESD have included projects to establish remote sensing centers in many countries and applications of remote sensing technologies for natural resource development.

—Center for Science and Technology for Development. It was established in 1979 as an organizationally distinct entity within the United Nations Secretariat. The center does not provide technical assistance to developing countries on an operational basis, but is involved in space activities in a number of ways. For instance, the center has undertaken activities aimed at establishing an international mechanism for the early assessment of space development implications.

—United Nations Development Program (UNDP). The UNDP administers and coordinates the great majority of the technical assistance provided through the UN system. The program has funded projects in areas of satellite broadcasting, satellites for telecommunication, remote sensing, aerial photography, and aerial surveys.

—United Nations Environment Program (UNEP). The UNEP was established in 1972. Its main interest in outer space activities is in remote sensing as an important tool for systematically collecting data on environmental problems. The data collection is carried out by the Global Environmental Monitoring System, which is coordinated by the UNEP Program Activity Center. The system itself is a concerted effort on the part of member states and other international organizations.

—Office of the United Nations Disaster Relief Coordinator (UNDRO). The UNDRO was established in 1971 to be the focal point for disaster relief and prevention in the UN system. In conjunction with the Centre National d'Études Spatiales (CNES) in Toulouse, France, since 1983 UNDRO has conducted a series of field trials of portable satellite transmitters. Since 1981, the Satellite Weather Bulletin Service of the National Oceanic and Atmospheric Administration of the United States has been installed at UNDRO, provided through the World Weather Watch program of the World Meteorological Organization (WMO).

—Economic and Social Commission for Asia and the Pacific (ESCAP). The objectives of the ESCAP Remote Sensing Program include provision of seminars, training courses, and workshops and the establishment of a regional information service.

—Economic Commission for Africa (ECA). The African Regional Remote Sensing Program is a regional cooperation program established in 1975 to make remote sensing techniques available to all state members of ECA.

Specialized Agencies of the United Nations

Food and Agriculture Organization (FAO) of the United Nations. FAO was established in 1945. In 1980, at the request of the Committee on the Peaceful Uses of Outer Space, FAO established a remote sensing center to cover remote sensing applications for renewable natural resources. The center, in consultation with FAO technical divisions, acts as the focal point for activities in space applications, particularly for aspects of agriculture, fisheries, and forestry.

United Nations Educational, Scientific, and Cultural Organization (UNESCO). UNESCO was established in 1945. The Sector for Communications of the Organization has two divisions that deal with satellites for communications. The Division of Development of Means of Communication is concerned with feasibility studies and training and production of appropriate low-cost broadcasting equipment relating to communication satellites. The division of Free Flow of Information and Communication Policies is responsible for all aspects of international exchange of information and television news and programs via communication satellites. In addition, the International Program for the Development of Communication examines and supports projects for the utilization of communication satellites within and between countries.

International Civil Aviation Organization (ICAO). ICAO was established in 1947. In 1968, the Air Navigation Commission established a panel of experts, the Application of Space Techniques Relating to Aviation (ASTRA) Panel, to pursue the technical interests of international civil aviation in space applications.

International Bank for Reconstruction and Development (IBRD). The IBRD was established in 1944. Two sections within the Bank deal with satellite imagery: the Economics and Resource Division of the Agriculture and Rural Development Department and the Cartographic Section of Administrative Services. The Economics and Resource Division is engaged in a variety of analytical work based on satellite data in computer tape form, whereas the Cartographic Section deals primarily with the film products and applications derived from those products. The work is carried out in connection with bank-financed projects in developing countries.

International Telecommunication Union (ITU). A large part of the work of ITU is related to the preparation and servicing of administrative radio conferences, at which are established the technical criteria and regulatory procedures to govern the use of frequency bands and radio communication services. The ITU is an international regulatory agency and it is involved in frequency assignment for all types of communications.

World Meteorological Organization (WMO). The activities of WMO relating to outer space come under the following programs of the organization:

1. World Weather Watch Program. Meteorological satellites constitute the space-based subsystem of the Global Observing System, to supplement the information provided by the ground-based subsystems in order to complete the global coverage.

2. World Climate Program. It consists of four different components: World Climate Applications Program, World Climate Data Program; World Climate Research Program, and World Climate Impacts Program.
3. Research and Development Program.
4. Application of Meteorology Program. The WMO Commission for Agricultural Meteorology provides member countries with practical guidance on satellite data that can be used in agriculture, forestry and the fight against desertification.
5. Hydrology and Water Resources Program. The WMO Commission for Hydrology is responsible for the development and use of applications of space technology to hydrology.

International Maritime Organization (IMO). The organization's main purpose is to facilitate cooperation among governments on technical matters affecting international shipping. Since 1966 IMO has taken part in the development and application of satellite technology at sea.

Other International or Intergovernmental Organizations

International Maritime Satellite Organization (INMARSAT). INMARSAT was established to meet the needs of international shipping for reliable communications. The purpose of the organization is to make provision for the space segment necessary for improving maritime communications. The organization either owns or leases the space segment and seeks to serve all geographical areas for the benefit of ships of all nations.

International Telecommunications Satellite Organization (INTELSAT). INTELSAT is a nonprofit cooperative of 131 countries that owns and operates the global communications satellite system, a system used by more than 180 countries, territories, and dependencies for international communications and by 27 countries for domestic communications.

International Organization of Space Communications (INTERSPUTNIK). INTERSPUTNIK was established to meet the demand of various countries for telephone and telegraph communications, exchange of radio and television programs, and transmission of other kinds of information in order to promote political, cultural, and economic cooperation among countries of the ex-communist block.

European Telecommunications Satellite Organization (EUTELSAT). The basic function of EUTELSAT is the design, development, construction, operation, and maintenance of the space segment of the European telecommunications satellite systems. The organization's prime objective is the provision of the space segment required for international public telecommunications services in Europe.

European Organization for the Exploitation of Meteorological Satellites (EUMETSAT). EUMETSAT is an intergovernmental organization of 16 European states. Its primary purpose is to establish, maintain, and exploit European systems of meteorological satellites.

Arab Satellite Communication Organization (ARABSAT). The main function of ARABSAT is to establish and maintain a regional telecommunications system for the Arab region. The system is intended to fulfill the aspiration of the Arabs in establishing their own satellite system as a means for socioeconomic development of the region.

Communication Satellite Corporation (COMSAT). COMSAT is a partly private, partly government-owned corporation established by the U.S. Congress with the *Communications Satellite Act of 1962* as the agency to spearhead the opening of the international satellite communications era. COMSAT is now a leading member of INTELSAT.

Individual Countries and Their Agencies[2]

It used to be that the United States and the Soviet Union had a virtual monopoly on space activities. The arms race of the cold war and the general rivalry of the two superpowers led to the development of sophisticated space systems and the growth of the aerospace industry in the two countries. It was not until much later that other nations sought to capitalize on the economic opportunities that the new frontier seemed to offer. The world of today is very different in the sense that most industrialized nations and even some developed countries are claiming their share of the economic benefits derived from aerospace activities. From the contractor's point of view, however, the government of the United States and the American industry still offer most of the opportunities, with Europe and Japan a distant second and third. The former Soviet Union, and particularly Russia, is still very much involved in the space business but the economic and political problems are so severe that the future is unpredictable.

Most European space programs are undertaken under the auspices of the European Space Agency (ESA), a Paris-based organization. ESA replaced the European Space Research Organization and the European Organization for the Development and Construction of Space Vehicle Launchers. It is basically a research and development (R&D) organization and does not develop and manufacture its own equipment. While the definition stages of a program are the responsibility of ESA's engineers and scientists working with experts from member states, development work proper is carried out by industry under the watchful eye of ESA's staff. An important aspect of the system is that it tries to ensure that each member state receives money back and has a share of the technological advances, in return for its investment in ESA. The system of contractual returns has been criticized, however, for hindering the efficient operation of ESA and its programs.

The countries of Europe which have invested the most in space activities are France, Germany, Italy and the United Kingdom. Other countries also have national space agencies but their programs are for the most part limited to their participation in the European Space Agency. The French CNES is the national agency responsible for the development of French space activities. The headquarters of the center are in Paris, the Launcher Division in Evry, the Space Center in Toulouse, and the launch range, which is also used by the European Space Agency, is in French Guyana. The activities of the center include space transportation, with Arianspace, earth observation with Spot Image, and many other sectors including space communications and funding and promoting of space technology.

Germany's space agency is Deutsche Agentur für Raumfahrtamgelegenheitgen (DARA), established in 1989. DARA's close partner in the implementation of space programs is the German Aerospace Research Establishment (DLR), whose space division deals with research and development work and is also largely responsible for the operational side of space projects. The Italian Space Agency (Agenzia) Spaziale Italiana, was established in 1988 and operates under the direction of the Ministry for the Coordination of Scientific and Technological Research. The British National Space Centre (BNSC) brings together the civil space interests of the British government and research councils. The BNSC is headquartered in London and has several technical centers, including the Royal Aerospace Establishment at Farnborough, Hampshire, and the Rutherford Appleton Laboratory at Chilton, Oxon.

As was noted earlier, the United States is still at the forefront of space activities from both a scientific and an economic point of view. The agencies of the U.S. government that deal with space are many and it would be beyond the scope of this book to attempt a detailed list. What follows is a brief mention of the major bodies involved.

NASA was established in 1958. It conducts research for the solution of flight problems within and outside the earth's atmosphere and develops, constructs, tests, and operates aeronautical and space vehicles. Within NASA there are several divisions. The Office of Aeronautics, Exploration, and Technology is responsible for the conduct of programs to develop advanced technology to enable and enhance the pursuit of national objectives in aeronautics, space and transatmospherics, including the National

Aerospace Plane program, if it is completed. The Office of Space Science and Applications is in charge of the administration's efforts to understand the origin, evolution, and structure of the universe, the solar system, and the integrated functioning of the earth. It conducts space application activities such as remote sensing of the earth. The Office of Space Flight (OSF) is responsible for providing the U.S. government civil space transportation and manned space-based facilities and operations in support of the NASA mission. OSF develops, operates, and maintains manned space-based facilities and space transportation systems and services. It is also in charge of managing the Johnson Space Center, Marshall Space Flight Center, Kennedy Space Center, and John C. Stennis Space Center. The office also plans the development of acquisition, testing, and operation of all elements of the space shuttle program. The Office of Space Operations is in charge of an array of functions critical to the operation of U.S. space programs. They include spacecraft operations and control centers, ground and space communications, data acquisition and processing, flight dynamics and trajectory analyses, and development of new technologies. Among NASA's field installations are the Ames Research Center, the Goddard Space Flight Center, the Jet Propulsion Laboratory, the Lyndon B. Johnson Space Center, the John F. Kennedy Space Center, the Langley Research Center, the Lewis Research Center, the George C. Marshall Space Flight Center, and the John C. Stennis Space Center.

The National Oceanic and Atmospheric Administration (NOAA) was established in 1970. NOAA's function is to explore, map, and chart the global ocean as well as to describe, monitor, and predict conditions in the atmosphere, ocean, Sun, and space environment. Among its principal activities, the administration provides satellite observations of the environment by operating a national environmental satellite system.

A very important regulatory organ is the Office of Commercial Space Transportation (OCST) of the Department of Transportation. It is in charge of licensing the private sector launchings of space payloads on expendable launch vehicles and commercial space launch facilities. The OCST also sets insurance requirements for the protection of persons and property and ensures that space transportation activities are in compliance with U.S. domestic and foreign policy.

The Federal Communications Commission regulates interstate and foreign communications by radio, television, wire, satellite, and cable. It is responsible for the coordinated development and operation of broadcast services and the provision of efficient national and worldwide telephone and telegraph services at reasonable rates. The Mass Media Bureau of the commission administers the regulatory program for radio, television, and direct satellite broadcasting. The Common Carrier Communications Bureau administers the regulatory program for interstate and international common carrier communications by telephone, telegraph, radio, and satellite.

The U.S. government investment on space-related activities in the fiscal year 1990 totaled over $30 billion. Most of these funds are divided between NASA and the Department of Defense (DoD), with the latter getting a little over $19 billion. The agencies and organs of the DoD that deal directly or indirectly with space activities are many. Together, they provide the world's largest space defense infrastructure.

In addition to the Army, and to a greater extent, the Air Force and the Navy, there are several agencies that make substantial use of satellites and other space-related services. The Defense Advanced Research Projects Agency engages in advanced basic and applied research and development projects and conducts prototype projects that embody technology that can be incorporated into joint programs or in support of selected military department programs. The Defense Informations Systems Agency is a combat support agency under the direction, authority, and control of the Assistant Secretary of Defense (Command, Control, Communications and Intelligence). The Defense Mapping Agency (DMA) generates computerized maps, charts, and operational data. Aerospace products and support to aerospace manned and unmanned weapons systems are provided to DoD users primarily by the DMA Aerospace Center. The National Security Agency (NSA) is responsible for the centralized coordination, direction, and performance of highly specialized, technical functions in support of U.S. government activities to protect U.S. communications and produce foreign intelligence information. The bulk of the NSA's operations is the collection of intelligence by means of sophisticated computers and extensive use of satellites.

THE LAWS

At the international level there are a number of agreements, including the following:

1. The *Treaty on Principles Governing the Exploration and Use of Outer Space Including the Moon and Other Celestial Bodies.* The agreement entered into force on October 10, 1968.
2. The *Agreement on the Rescue of Astronauts, Return of Astronauts, and the Return of Objects Launched into Outer Space*, which entered into force on December 3, 1968.

3. The *Convention on International Liability for Damage Caused by Space Objects*, which entered into force on September 15, 1972.
4. The *Convention on the Registration of Objects Launched into Outer Space*, which entered into force on September 15, 1976.
5. The *Agreement Governing the Activities of States on the Moon and Other Celestial Bodies*, which entered into force in July of 1984.

Those treaties constitute the bulk of what is referred to as "space law," intended as that branch of public international law that deals with activities that take place beyond the atmosphere. From a practical point of view, the effect of these treaties is somewhat limited for several reasons. First of all, not all treaties have been ratified by the major space powers, which means that they are not binding on them. A treaty that does not bind Russia and the United States, for example, has little practical significance because most space activities are conducted by those two countries. The other main reason for the limited practical effect of those treaties is that they mostly deal with issues of principle and not with the day-to-day activities of aerospace companies.

The previously listed agreements were drafted at a time when space activities were almost exclusively a government endeavor. Little effort was therefore made to accommodate the needs of private entrepreneurs. Beginning with the Carter administration and increasingly with the Reagan administration, the dominant philosophy in space development shifted toward private initiative.[3] Some industries have been privatized, some deregulated, and others assisted. NASA and the Air Force were required to help private companies use government launch facilities at low prices.

Private industry is mostly concerned with private law, which is increasingly important in space activities. Traditional private law includes contracts, torts, real and personal property, corporations, secured transactions, insurance, and many other fields. Gradually, several of these branches of law are becoming applicable to space endeavors. Although the most important legal issues are discussed in the chapters that follow, a brief mention of U.S. legislation is given here for general reference.

Procurement by the U.S. government is mostly regulated by the *Federal Acquisition Regulations* (FAR). The FAR system sets uniform policies and procedures for acquisition by all executive agencies. In addition, there are internal agency guidance procedures issued pursuant to Section 48 of the *Code of Federal Regulations.* Supplementing the FAR are the *Defense Acquisition Regulations*, which govern the Department of Defense and its various agencies. The Army, Navy, Air Force, and some other defense agencies also have their own regulations to supplement the *Defense Acquisition Regulations*. Disputes arising under contracts entered into by federal agencies for the procurement of property or services are governed by the *Contract Disputes Act of 1978*. Other applicable statutes include the *Administrative Procedure Act* and the *Tucker Act*.

In order to deal with the issues involved in commercial space agreements, the Air Force and the National Aeronautics and Space Administration have developed their own set of rules. The Air Force has developed a *Model Expendable Launch Vehicle Commercialization Agreement* to serve as the standard type of contract for all commercial users of the facilities under its control at Patrick Air Force Base, Florida, and Vandenberg Air Force Base, California. For the same type of contractual situation NASA, which also uses a sample contract, prefers to deal individually with the users of its facilities at Cape Canaveral, Florida; Wallops Island, Virginia; and other sites.

A statute of major importance for space commerce is the *Commercial Space Launch Act* of 1984 and its 1988 amendments. The act designates the Department of Transportation as the lead agency for commercial launch activities. Pursuant to the act, the department is now in charge of (1) licensing and regulating all U.S. launch activities and ensuring that they are conducted safely and (2) promoting, encouraging, and facilitating space transportation.

Satellite communications are subject to a complex regulatory system, both national and international. At the international level, the International Telecommunications Union has the overall responsibility for the assignment of frequencies to individual countries. At the U.S. level, the Federal Communications Commission (FCC) is the regulatory agency pursuant to the *Communications Act* of 1934. In fulfilling its mandate, the FCC follows the *Commission Rules* and the *Commission Decisions*. Secured financing, as it may apply to space activity assets that must serve as collateral for loans, is governed for the most part by the *Uniform Commercial Code*, and particularly by Article 9.

Intellectual property, which is mostly an international issue, is governed by several treaties. Trademarks are dealt with by the:

1. *Madrid Agreement Concerning the International Registration of Marks*;
2. *Trademark Registration Treaty*;
3. *Nice Agreement Concerning the International Classification of Goods and Services for the Purpose of the Registration of Marks*;

4. *Vienna Agreement Establishing an International Classification of the Figurative Elements of Marks*; and
5. *Lisbon Agreement for the Protection of Appellations of Origin.*

Patent protection has also been the subject of several international treaties. The United Nations treaties listed at the beginning of this section do not deal with the protection of private interests and intellectual property rights. They contain, however, some general statements of principle that can have the effect of limiting certain types of intellectual rights protection. They are discussed in detail in the chapters that follow. Among the other international treaties are the following:

1. Paris Convention for the Protection of Industrial Property;
2. Patent Cooperation Treaty; and
3. Strasbourg Convention on the International Classification of Patents.

At the domestic level, the relevant statutes are the *Inventions Security Act*, the *Patents Law Amendments Act of 1984*, and the *Space Patent Act of 1990*. Of these, the *Space Patent Act* is the most important because it specifically extends protection to inventions used or sold on a space object.

The protection of copyrighted works transmitted by satellite has posed a challenge to the international community for three decades because the *International Telecommunication Convention* and the *Radio Regulations of the International Telecommunications Union* are considered inadequate, as are the *Universal Copyright Convention* and the *Berne Convention for the Protection of Literary and Artistic Works*. The legislative gap was addressed by the *Convention Relating to the Distribution of Program-Carrying Signals Transmitted by Satellite*, which entered into force in 1979 and was ratified by the United States in 1984.

Because of the large size of many aerospace companies in a very specialized industry, antitrust issues assume great importance. That is so particularly in the 1990s with the reduction in defense spending and the consequent restructuring, consolidation, and mergers of many companies. In the United States, the most important statutes dealing with antitrust are the *Sherman Act* and the *Clayton Act*. In order to mitigate the effects of U.S. antitrust legislation, which placed American companies at a competitive disadvantage in the international market, the *National Cooperative Research Act* was enacted in 1984. Other legislation designed to address the problems of unfair trade practices includes the *Tariff Act of 1930* and the *Trade Act of 1974*.

In the field of technology transfer, there are several statutes that should be mentioned. The *Stevenson-Wydler Technology Innovation Act of 1980* established and funded offices of research and technology applications. The *Small Business Innovation and Development Act of 1982* required federal agencies to develop small business innovation research programs. The *National Defense Authorization Act of 1987* encouraged the secretary of defense to promote domestic technology transfer of technology developed by the Department of Defense. A *1987 Executive Order Facilitating Access to Science and Technology* called on the secretary of defense to identify new technologies that could be useful to U.S. industries. The *Omnibus Trade and Competitiveness Act of 1988* changed the name of the National Bureau of Standards to the National Institute of Standards and Technology (NIST) to reflect NIST's broadened role of promoting the commercialization of federally developed technology. The *Federal Technology Transfer Acts of 1986 and 1989* mandated greater efforts to transfer technology from the public to the private sector.

Aerospace products for both military and civilian use tend to move across international boundaries more than most other goods. A satellite, for example, can be built in one country and launched from another with components from yet another country. For national security reasons, however, the export of certain goods and technologies is regulated at both the national and international levels. In the United States, the main legislation dealing with export controls is the *Export Administration Act*, the *Arms Export Control Act*, and the *International Traffic in Arms Regulation*. Internationally, export controls by Western nations are mostly governed by the *COCOM Procedures* (Coordinating Committee on Multilateral Export Controls).

NOTES

1. For more information on international agencies see, in general, George V. d'Angelo, *Aerospace Agencies and Organizations: A Guide for Business and Government*, Quorum Books, Westport, Conn., 1993.
2. *Id.*
3. Nathan Goldman, *American Space Law*, Iowa University Press, Ames, 1988, at 115.

Chapter Two

Contracts

GENERAL FEATURES OF COMMERCIAL SPACE CONTRACTS

This chapter discusses some contractual issues relevant to the field of aerospace activities. The term *aerospace contracts* is quite broad but, in this context, it is meant to encompass a wide range of agreements, including space equipment sale and lease agreements, such as satellites and transponder purchase contracts, launch service agreements, and other related issues. General procurement procedures are dealt with in Chapter 3.

Commercial space contracts, as this field of law is also known, should be no different from contracts in any other domain in the sense that agreements are no more than the will of two or more parties translated into a written, clear, more or less permanent form. Yet there are many elements involved in space transactions, mostly related to high technology, that add important features to these agreements and render them quite unique.

Imprecision in contract wording, which often has the effect of shifting risk or liability from one party to the other, becomes particularly dangerous in a highly specialized field such as aerospace. The same can be said about ambiguity due to lack of familiarity with the risks involved in space projects.

Ever since space manufacturers and service providers have sought to limit or disclaim liability, their customers have sought to impose progressively higher levels of responsibility. Although the traditional argument that space is a high-risk area has lost some credit, the magnitude of the exposure and insurance costs remain significant.[1] No matter how carefully a liability limitation provision or disclaimer is drafted, it is always possible to challenge it. As will be seen later, in satellite purchase contracts, the point at which risk passes cannot be stressed enough.

Every commercial space contract has an express governing law provision. The interpretation of disclaimer provisions, however, can vary from state to state. In international satellite projects, one party often insists that its law apply. The selection of applicable law can have an important impact on the outcome of any dispute. When the operative language is not English the uncertainties are even greater. In certain cases it becomes extremely important to seek the advice of local counsel.[2]

GOVERNMENT CONTRACTS

The very nature of the aerospace business makes governments and, particularly, the government of the United States and its agencies, a major player and sometimes indispensable customer. It is therefore essential to examine some aspects and special features of government contracts. Despite the obvious similarities between government contracts and those between private parties, there are substantial differences worthy of close inspection.

Generally, government contracts are different from those between private parties because of the sovereign character of the government and certain sovereign acts, which can interfere with the performance of its duties and for which it can be unaccountable. More specifically, the two major differences are the "changes" clause and the option to terminate a contract for convenience of the government.[3] A change order is a written order signed by the contracting officer directing the contractor to make a change authorized by the changes clause, an action which in a private agreement would amount to breach of contract. The authority of the government to terminate a contract in the public interest when services or supplies are no longer needed (for convenience of the government) was established by a Supreme Court decision.[4] In the aerospace field, most government contracts are quite different from standard U.S. government contracts. This is true particularly for launch facility use agreements.

Commercial space launch facility use agreements are contracts between NASA or the other agencies that manage the federal government's space launch facilities and private users or contractors. Unlike most traditional contracts entered into by the U.S. government, the government sells or leases property or services to private industry instead of the other way around.[5]

The *Contract Disputes Act* of 1978[6] does not apply to the government's launch facility use agreements. The act, by its terms, governs disputes arising under contracts entered into by federal agencies for the procurement of property, or services. The *Contract Disputes Act*[7] does not extend to the sale of services, property, or other items by the government, with the limited exception of disposal of personal property. Similarly, the *Federal Acquisition Regulations*[8] is inapplicable to the government's launch facility use agreements since that regulation governs the acquisition of services or supplies by the federal government.

The Air Force and the National Aeronautics and Space Administration have developed their own set of rules in order to deal with the type of issues involved in commercial space agreements. The Air Force has developed a "*Model Expendable Launch Vehicle Commercialization Agreement*" to serve as the standard type of contract for all commercial users of the facilities under its control at Patrick Air Force Base, Florida, and Vandenberg Air Force Base, California. The actual contracts entered into by the Air Force for launch facility use follow this prototype with minimal variations. NASA has chosen instead to deal individually with the users of its facilities at Cape Canaveral, Florida; Wallops Island, Virginia; and other sites. It appears that NASA's contracts actually vary considerably from one another.[9]

The actual contractual provisions used by NASA and the Air Force are quite different particularly with regard to disputes and remedies. Article IX of the Air Force Model Agreement sets forth a four-step dispute settlement procedure:

- the Air Force and the contractor are first expected to attempt to resolve any dispute by agreement;
- disputes not disposed of by agreement of the parties are to be decided by the Air Force Commercial Services Contracting Officer, who must issue a written decision within 60 days after receiving a written claim;
- the decision of the Commercial Services Contracting Officer will be final and conclusive, unless within thirty days of its receipt the contractor seeks review by the Armed Services Board of Contract Appeals;
- the decision of the Armed Services Board of Contract Appeals will be final and conclusive "concerning questions of fact" unless determined by a U.S. court of competent jurisdiction to have been "fraudulent or capricious, or arbitrary, or so grossly erroneous as necessarily to imply bad faith, or not supported by substantial evidence."[10]

By contrast, NASA's sample contract,[11] at article IX, provides for a more complex dispute settlement procedure. The basic elements are the following:

- any disputes must be referred to designated field representatives of the parties for attempted resolution;
- in case the field representatives cannot reach agreement, the "claimant" can refer the dispute in writing to the NASA Associate Administrator for Space Flight and the contractor's signatory to this Agreement;
- if these officials cannot resolve the dispute within 30 days after receiving notice of it, the NASA Associate Administrator must then issue a written decision within 10 days;
- within 30 days of receiving written notice of that decision, the contractor may appeal the matter to the NASA Board of Contract Appeals;
- the NASA Board of Contract Appeals "shall afford the parties an opportunity to be heard and to offer evidence" and will then issue "proposed findings of fact and conclusions of law"; and
- the proposed resolution of the NASA board is then sent to the Administrator of NASA "or his designee," who must within 60 days either adopt or reject the board's proposal. If the administrator rejects the proposal, he must issue a written decision of his own, which must include his reasons for not adopting the board's findings and conclusions. If the administrator fails to act within 60 days, the board's proposed resolution will become the final agency decision;
- the final agency decision "will be conclusive as to all issues and binding on the parties unless overturned by a court of competent jurisdiction."

Both the NASA sample contract and the Air Force Model Agreement do not state which court is competent to review the agencies' final decisions. It would seem that, if the remedy sought is damages subject to the *Tucker Act*,[12] the U.S. Claims Court could take jurisdiction. If the request is for equitable relief from a final agency decision under the *Administrative Procedure Act*,[13] the appeal would normally be taken to a U.S. District Court.[14]

It is not clear which would be the law applicable to the disputes arising under the aforementioned contracts. The Air Force Model Agreement states that "United States law" shall govern, and the NASA sample contract provides that "United States Federal Law" will apply for all purposes, but neither one explains what that law would be. Courts would probably decide on the applicable law on a case-by-case basis.

Neither the NASA Sample Contract nor the Air Force Model Agreement uses the standard government contract provisions on termination for convenience and for default. The launch facility use agreements use instead a form of termination for cause clauses, giving the government agencies the contractual rights to terminate for certain specifically enumerated reasons.

Article VIII of NASA's Sample Contract provides the following grounds for termination:

1. a declaration of war by Congress or of a national emergency by the president;
2. a failure by the contractor to make payments as specified in the contract;
3. a "NASA determination in writing" that it cannot provide the agreed services for reasons beyond its control "which make impractical or impossible NASA's or its contractors' or its subcontractors' performance" under the contract; and
4. a breach by the contractor of a provision in this Agreement. In such case NASA may terminate its performance "in whole or in part."

If NASA terminates the contract for any of the first three reasons, it will not be liable for any costs of the contractor. The contractor, however, will be liable for (i) the cost of fixed-price property or services that "would have been provided had termination not taken place"; (ii) all costs for property or services provided on a cost basis; and (iii) termination costs. In case of termination pursuant to number four, "NASA's rights shall be in accordance with law."

Article XIV of the Air Force Model Agreement provides that the agency can terminate the contract after 30 days of the contractor's receipt of written notice on the following grounds:

1. the contractor abandons or discontinues commercial space transportation operations, and there is no evidence that such operations will be resumed within a reasonable time;
2. the contractor fails, despite notice, to conduct its operations in a safe manner;
3. the contractor is in arrears in its payments;
4. requirements develop for "critical, conflicting national security or other governmental launch activities"; and
5. the contractor fails or refuses, after 30 days written notice, to comply with any material provision of the agreement. This provision does not give the Air Force the right to effect a partial termination.

When, for any of the preceding reasons the Air Force elects to terminate the contract, the Model Agreement provides that the Air Force will not be liable for any costs incurred by the contractor. The contractor, however, must "reimburse the government for all direct costs incurred up to the effective date of termination." The Agreement defines direct cost as the "actual costs that can be unambiguously associated with a commercial launch effort and would not be borne by the United States government in the absence of a commercial launch."[15]

The *Commercial Space Launch Act* and its 1988 amendments require the execution of "reciprocal waivers" by the Department of Transportation and all launch licensees and their contractors, subcontractors, and customers.[16] Under these reciprocal waivers, each party must assume responsibility for any loss or property damage it sustains from activities carried out under a launch license issued by the Department of Transportation (DOT). Both the Air Force and NASA, however, use contract provisions aimed at imposing on launch contractors certain responsibilities for damage to government property and for third-party liability. Article IV of the Air Force Model Agreement provides that a contractor is responsible for:

- all damage to government property, "in accordance with the Commercial Space Launch Act as amended," in the case of activities carried out under a DOT license; otherwise, with respect to unlicensed launch activities, all damage to government property, regardless of fault;
- all damage to the contractor, whether resulting from activities carried out under a license or not, except as waived by DOT or resulting from the "reckless disregard or wilful misconduct of the United States or its agents"; and
- all third party liability, "in accordance with the Commercial Space Launch Act as amended," resulting from activities carried out under a DOT launch license; otherwise, with respect to unlicensed launch activities, all third-party liability, regardless of fault.

Under the Sample Contract of NASA, the U.S. government waives any claim for property damage in excess of the insurance limits established in the contract.[17] The contractor is also required, in addition to providing insurance protection, to indemnify the government and its contractors from liability for damage to a launch vehicle, its payload, or any other property of the contractor.[18] The government also reserves the right to bring an action against "any responsible party" for any third-party liability against the government in excess of the government insurance limits.[19] Article VI also provides[20] that the insurance coverage purchased by the contractor may exclude damage caused by the U.S. government's willful misconduct or reckless disregard.

Both the Air Force Model Agreement and the NASA Sample Contract permit government agencies to pursue ordinary contract remedies to the extent not covered by a Launch Act waiver. The NASA Sample Contract, however, poses an important restriction: the contractor's liability "shall be limited to direct damages only and shall not include any loss of revenue, profits or other indirect or consequential damages."[21]

The rights of contractors to terminate the contract are different in the Model Agreement and the Sample Contract that we have examined. The Air Force Model Agreement provides that the contractor can terminate the contract without cause "at any time" by providing written notice to the Air Force Commercial Services Contracting Officer.[22] If this right is exercised, however, the contractor must reimburse the Air Force for (i) all direct costs incurred by the government at the date of termination notice, (ii) all direct costs incurred by the government in restoring the launch facility and equipment to the previous condition, and (iii) other termination costs resulting directly from the termination.[23] The Air Force also reserves the right to pursue any additional remedies provided elsewhere in the agreement or by law.[24] The Model Agreement is silent with respect to the contractor's right to terminate the contract for fault of the Air Force. Presumably, this leaves the contractor free to pursue its common law rights if there is a breach by the Air Force. Assuming that the contractor could overcome any sovereign immunity defense, it could seek not only its actual damages but also incidental and consequential damages.[25] Under the NASA Sample Contract, the contractor has the right to terminate the contract for convenience at any time, in whole or in part.[26] Advance or written notice is not required but the contractor is responsible for reimbursing the government for all costs that have been incurred up to the effective date of the termination and are incurred as a result of the termination.[27] The Sample Contract provides that the contractor may terminate for NASA's breach "of a provision of this agreement" but recoverable damages are limited to direct damages only and do not include any loss of revenue, profits, and other indirect or consequential damages.[28]

The government has attempted in a variety of ways to limit the right of commercial users of its launch facilities to recover damages against it. The discussed termination provisions have the overall effect of limiting the recoverable damages. The *Commercial Space Launch Act* requires the execution of reciprocal waivers. The launch act also provides that the government can preempt or cancel a commercial launch in cases of "imperative national need."[29] If that were to happen, the launch agency is required to attempt to reschedule the launch and may not charge the contractor for tests and other services necessary to reschedule a launch.[30] The reciprocal waiver required by the Launch Act, however, would make it difficult for the contractor to seek reimbursement from the government for any additional expenses sustained as a result of a canceled launch. The Air Force Model Agreement also provides that the government has first priority in the use of government property and support services to meet "national security interests or U.S. government mission requirements." The decision to exercise the government priority right would be made by the Center Commander at Patrick Air Force Base or Vanderberg Air Force Base as the case may be.[31] The Air Force may exercise that right and interrupt the facility user's schedule without liability for any damages or costs caused by the interruption.[32] NASA also has a priority right to use government property and services under article X of its Sample Contract. That contract, however, does not preclude a contractor from seeking reimbursement for expenses incurred as a result of any government-caused delay or interruption, provided that the Launch Act waiver can be avoided. With regard to government property made available to a contractor, neither NASA nor the Air Force agreements make any express or implied warranties and the property is offered "as is."[33] If the government does not raise the sovereign immunity defense and the reciprocal waiver provision can be circumvented, a contractor could still bring an action for breach of contract and at least recover the actual damages.

SATELLITE AGREEMENTS IN GENERAL

The commercial satellite industry has many players: manufacturers of satellites; launchers of satellites; owners and operators of satellites; owners, lessors, or lessees of transponder capacity; providers of services delivered by satellite; and the service industry supporting satellite providers. The service industry includes financial institutions and investors, insurers, accountants, lawyers, and many others. Booming as the communications industry may be, the satellite business is still somewhat unique in that it involves large investments and high risk. For example, there is always a substantial risk that a satellite may not make it into space due to a failed launch or malfunction. Even when the launch is successful, there could be improper deployment in space or malfunction of the satellite itself, which would leave the satellite idle. Currently only the Space Shuttle of the United States can repair, service, or retrieve and redeploy a satellite. The backlog for use of the shuttle, however, would delay redeployment of a satellite by several years.[34]

The purchase or lease of a satellite and related equipment is far from being just another equipment procurement. There must be provisions describing the scope of work and a detailed statement of work. There is a price and payment schedule. There may be a price of profit incentives tied to reduced costs, expedited completion, or successful in-orbit performance. There is the ever present concern of risk allocation.[35]

Purchasers strive for a contract that transfers absolutely all of the risk to the satellite manufacturer. They would like the manufacturer to build the spacecraft, arrange for the launch, and assume the launch risks as well as warrant correct deployment and the proper functioning of the satellite. Obviously, manufacturers are unwilling to agree to this type of arrangement, unless they can charge an outrageous premium for the additional risk they bear. Usually, manufacturers want to terminate their risk at some precise point, typically the intentional ignition of the launch vehicle.

The procurement contract should specify that, prior to launch, the manufacturer will insure the spacecraft during construction, transit, integration, and storage. The purchaser should insist on a provision granting him the right to review and approve the insurance policy. The agreement should also require the manufacturer to assume all third-party liabilities during the manufacturing, storage, and transportation phases for negligence of the manufacturer. A provision should be included requiring the manufacturer to indemnify the purchaser for any liabilities incurred due to the negligence or default of the manufacturer or its subcontractors during these stages. The purchaser should also insist on a provision on indemnification from the manufacturer for additional costs resulting from a delayed launch caused by late delivery of a spacecraft.[36]

At the point when the purchaser assumes the real risk, which is ordinarily at the time of launch, there are two main concerns: insuring the spacecraft itself and providing for the cost of any replacement launch. In most launch service contracts, the launching entity usually only promises "best efforts," which is a strong incentive for the purchaser to buy insurance. Even if the launch is successful the purchaser wants the satellite to work. The manufacturer, however, usually only warrants that the spacecraft will be free of defects at the time of launch, when risk usually transfers to the purchaser. In order to solve this problem, the purchaser should include in the contract "incentives" or "performance payments" to be paid to the manufacturer if the spacecraft operates in good order. Alternatively, the contract could require the manufacturer to return a portion of the procurement cost in the event of inadequate performance or failure.[37]

The negotiation process in the purchase or lease of a satellite transponder is just as tricky as the purchase of the satellite itself and involves a variety of preparatory steps. Drafting an agreement to fit the particular needs and desires of the user is critical and may mean the difference between success or failure of the venture.[38] Perhaps more than in other sectors of aerospace commerce, users of satellites and transponders should seek out competent engineering advice to determine system requirements and the means to meet those needs.

The transponder agreement should specify the transponder number, C band or Ku band, bandwidth in megahertz, satellite beam for transponder location, and service limitation provisions. If the capacity is a 36 MHz portion of a 72 MHz transponder, the satellite operator should specify whether the other portion is shared with another customer, and if so, whom and type of usage. For satellites that are already operational, the user should demand transponder-specific service specifications based on actual satellite performance measurements. When measuring the satellite's performance, the parties should insist on both a location and a technique for measurement. Predictions of signal strength and coverage should be avoided whenever possible. It is a good idea to include in a service agreement a glossary of defined technical terms to avoid disputes later.[39]

Satellite operators should warrant the estimated useful life of the satellite and the technical ability of the transponder at least through the life of the contract. If telemetry, tracking, and control (TTC) services are provided by other than the capacity supplier, the TTC contract term should also be guaranteed by the supplier.[40] Satellite capacity suppliers should also warrant all necessary government permits and licenses for service supply. If uplink services are included, the transmitting earth station should be licensed to or have a contractual commitment to the supplier. Renewal passages should be included in the service agreement if the earth station license expires during the term of the agreement. In international service agreements, the supplier should guarantee signal reception in the designated downlink country. Contingencies should also be provided for loss of downlinking rights during the life of the agreement or if downlinking rights will be obtained from countries with which no downlinking agreements currently exist, with respect to the satellite signal.[41]

An essential element of the transponder agreement is the precise formulation of the respective rights and obligations of the parties in the event of an interruption in service or total satellite failure. Agreements should provide for outage and/or degraded service credits and specify the backup capacity switching rights. It is important, however, to establish clear and realistic criteria for the determination of the onset and duration of any interruption. Agreements should also make clear that degraded service or frequent service outages constitutes a ground for premature termination of the agreement. Language should be included to the effect that the supplier use its best efforts to restore the signal to the specifications established by the parties.[42]

Transponder agreements should establish objective criteria for the switch-over rights to spare capacity in order to determine supplier obligations of transfer to a spare transponder. The prudent user will check the order of transfer rights in the event the satellite experiences the simultaneous failure of several transponders. It is also important to examine the specifications of spare transponders to see if they differ from the original transponder. The contract should specify which party pays incidental costs for the relocation, such as earth station repointing costs for an off-satellite spare as well as customer information costs.[43]

The problem with transponder substitution is that it is difficult to assess transponder availability in the future. Users who require continued service must include in the contract some form of successor rights provision that guarantees renegotiation rights for comparable capacity on a successor or replacement satellite. At the very least, a successor rights provision should specify a negotiation window close enough to the term of the original agreement so that the user can make an informed business projection of future needs. There should also be a provision in the contract for the transfer of existing service onto a successor satellite if the satellites' operational lives overlap.[44]

THE STANDARD SATELLITE PURCHASE CONTRACT

As noted earlier, agreements relating to activities in the field of aerospace are quite unique. Contracts for the purchase of satellites also have to address very specific issues not encountered in other types of hardware procurement, and each one of those agreements tends to be the result of individual negotiations. There are, however, a number of issues that are present in most satellite purchase contracts and result in a standard set of provisions.[45]

The first provision in any spacecraft purchase agreement should be a statement of the scope of work to be provided as well as the delivery schedule. The manufacturer may be required to provide one or more satellites. It may also provide for the manufacture of a spare satellite, in which case provision should be made for storage on the ground. The actual specific requirements are usually detailed in schedules or exhibits to the general terms and conditions of the agreement.

Another essential provision regards the price and payment terms. These terms are often the result of extensive negotiations and are usually linked to the delivery schedule. Typically, the purchaser of a satellite is not going to earn any revenues until the satellite is operational; that is, built, launched, and activated. Until then, there are only expenses. In order to mitigate these huge up front costs government agencies often make export financing available, which is designed to stimulate the sale of domestically manufactured equipment. In the United States Eximbank (Export-Import Bank of the United States) can provide this type of financing. In France the agency is

Compagnie Française d'Assurance pour le Commerce Extérieur) (COFACE).

A third provision is excusable delays. Usually, the manufacturer will not assume any responsibilities for delays that result from acts beyond its reasonable control such as acts of God, fire, flood, earthquake, government acts, and other unforeseeable events. As in most types of contracts, excusable delays will result in an equitable adjustment of the time for performance.

Title and risk of loss is an essential provision. It is usually the manufacturer that will assume all risk of loss of the equipment until intentional ignition of the first stage engines of the launch vehicle. Any loss or damage occurring after ignition or launch will normally be borne by the purchaser.

A fifth provision regards licenses, permits, and other government approvals. As discussed in other chapters, space activities are regulated by several agencies and a complex set of laws. In the case of a communication satellite, for example, in addition to other relevant permits, the Federal Communication Commission imposes a whole set of requirements. In a satellite purchase agreement, the responsibility for such permits is divided between the manufacturer and the customer. Typically, the manufacturer will be responsible for the permits that are necessary for the construction and delivery of the equipment. The purchaser will be responsible for the licenses required for the launch and operation of the satellite as well as launch site activities.

A provision that is almost always present is that of indemnification. The manufacturer and the seller typically agree to indemnify and hold harmless the other for loss and injury that arise before launch and results from the performance of work. Pursuant to this provision, if during the manufacturing process an injury or damage is caused by the manufacturer to the customer or vice versa, the party responsible will indemnify and hold harmless the other.

Performance warranties, as in other types of contracts, are designed to spell out performance specifications and are subject to extensive negotiation. They tend to vary from project to project.

Multiple satellite procurement usually requires provisions designed to correct defects in an unlaunched satellite. The typical provision requires that, in the event the first satellite to be manufactured does not operate according to specifications, the manufacturer will be responsible for affecting corrective measures for subsequent satellites to ensure they will be free of defects.

Spacecraft purchase agreements often include provisions dealing with intellectual property. Normally, the manufacturer will retain all patent and intellectual property rights arising in connection with the manufacture of the satellite. The purchaser, however should expect to be indemnified for any claims of patent infringement resulting from the manufacturing process.

A typical provision in satellite contracts regards storage. If there is a launch delay, the satellite may need to be stored until the launch is available. Also, if the contract involves an on-ground spare, the spare satellite needs to be stored pending launch in the event of an in-orbit satellite failure. There is no standard allocation of storage expenses. As with many other provisions, the parties negotiate the terms according to specific situations.

Given the enormous costs involved in satellite projects and the risks involved, the parties to a satellite purchase agreement may wish to include insurance provisions in the contract.

Provisions regarding inspection and acceptance, access to work in progress and other similar terms are details that the parties must carefully negotiate on an individual basis. Other terms a satellite purchase agreement would include, such as the choice of law, the arbitration clause, and others, are no different from other types of contracts and therefore are not discussed here.

NOTES

1. Peter. D. Nesgos, *Lessons Learned in Negotiating Space Contracts*, address of March 12, 1993, at the Seventh Assicurazioni Gnerali Space Insurance Conference, Rome, Italy, p. 2.
2. *Id.*, p. 5.
3. Paul G. Dembling, Introduction to Panel III: *Contract Issues*, in 4 Journal of Law and Technology, 1989, p. 29.
4. United States v. Corliss Steam-Engine Co., 91 U.S. 321 (1875).
5. See Ralph L. Kissick, *Commercial Space Launch Contracts: Disputes and Remedies*, 4 Journal of Law and Technology, 1989, pp. 31 *et seq.*
6. 41 U.S.C. pars. 601–613 (1982).
7. 41 U.S.C. par. 602 (1982).
8. 48 C.F.R. pts. 1–53 (1988).
9. See Kissick, *supra*, p. 32.
10. Air Force Model Agreement art. IX pars. a and b.
11. Contract of October 1988 between NASA and Martin Marietta Commercial Titan, Inc.
12. 28 U.S.C. paras. 1346–1491(a)(1) (1982).
13. 5 U.S.C. paras. 701–704 (1982); 28 U.S.C. para. 1331(a) (1982).
14. See Kissick, *supra*, p. 35.
15. Air Force Model Agreement art. III.
16. 49 U.S.C. par. 2615(a)(1)(D) (1988).
17. NASA Sample Contract, art. VI, § 3 c.
18. *Id.*, § 2.d.

19. *Id.*
20. *Id.*, § 3.b.
21. Air Force Model Agreement, art. XIV, § b.
22. *Id.*
23. *Id.*, at § a.
24. *Id.*, art XIII § b.
25. See Kissick, *supra*, p. 39.
26. NASA Sample Contract, art. VIII, § 4.
27. *Id.*
28. *Id.*, art. VI § 5.
29. 49 U.S.C., *supra* § 2614 (b)(4)(A) (1988).
30. *Id.*, at §§ 2614(b)(4) (A), (B).
31. Air Force Model Agreement, art. XII, § b.
32. *Id.* at § c.
33. NASA Sample Contract, art. IV, § 3; Air Force Model Agreement, art. IV, § d.
34. See Tazewell Ellett, Moderator, Introduction to Panel I: *Satellite Provider Legal Issues*, 5 Journal of Law and Technology, 1990, pp. 9–10.
35. Joel S. Winnik, *Risk Allocation in Spacecraft Procurement Contracts*, Journal of Law and Technology, *supra*, p. 13.
36. *Id.*, p. 14.
37. *Id.*, p. 15.
38. See Raul R. Rodriguez and Stephen D. Baruch, *Satellite Sales and Lease Agreements: A User's Guide*, Satellite Communications, July 1990, p. 15.
39. *Id.*
40. *Id.*
41. *Id.*, p. 16.
42. *Id.*
43. *Id.*
44. *Id.*, p. 17.
45. See Peter Nesgos, *Legal Aspects of Space Commercialization. Contract and Insurance Issues in Telecommunications Satellite Projects,* remarks at the International Space University, 1992 Summer Session, Kitakyushu, Japan, August 11, 1992.

Chapter Three

Government and International Agency Procurement

For all that is said about commercialization of space, the bulk of activities in the field still depends on direct or indirect government financing and participation. Space activities, with the possible exception of telecommunication satellites, are not yet commercially viable in terms of rate of return on capital investment. The risks are too many and the time span involved in most space projects is too long to justify the magnitude of investment required by those activities.

Both military and peaceful uses of space, such as space exploration, are commissioned by or financed in large part by governments directly or through international agencies and a variety of programs.[1] Space commerce or space business is therefore closely linked to government not only in terms of regulatory matters but for the funding of space activities itself, without which the aerospace industry would not even exist. For that reason, in examining business law aspects of aerospace activities, it is imperative to have an understanding of government procurement practices.

This chapter examines some aspects of procurement by national governments and some international organizations. It is by no means intended to cover all laws and regulations of all states. The goal is to give a general idea of what is involved in government acquisition practices from the point of view of the contractor. As in other chapters, we shall see some familiar provisions as well as practices unique to the aerospace field.

THE UNITED NATIONS

Procurement by international organizations is a field of great economic significance but quite unique in many aspects. Such procurement activities are international in terms of the procuring agency, the suppliers, and the products. They are often conducted outside the framework of national legislation and are governed by an independent set of regulations and practices. They usually involve long-term advanced technology projects with a research and development element. Last but not least, political considerations tend to influence all stages of the procurement process.[2]

In accordance with the Financial Regulations and Rules of the United Nations, procurement by the United Nations is basically carried out through (a) a Request for Proposal; (b) the terms of reference for the specific proposal; (c) the General Conditions of Contract; and (d) the actual contract, which incorporates by reference the general conditions.

A contract for the procurement of goods or services for a project executed by the United Nations contains some standard provisions described below.

In case of any inconsistencies among the various documents constituting the contract, the following order of priority applies: (1) the agreement and the UN General Conditions; (2) the Request for Proposal; (3) the Proposal.

Under the heading of responsibilities of the contractor the agreement imposes a duty on the contractor to use all necessary professional care in the performance of the contract and in the preparation of its reports and recommendations. The UN relies on the contractor's expertise as described in the Proposal and the government involved relies on the recommendations of the contractor. The agreement specifies the use of a certain number of personnel and the man-months of their employment. For example, project managers, special advisers, project secretaries, and other key personnel are allocated a number of man-months. The contractor is under an obligation to provide suitable replacements in the event that some specified employees become unavailable. Additional descriptions of duties are added for team leaders of the project.

A schedule of work includes the date for the commencement of work and follow-up in the case, for example, of satellite imaging. The contractor is to submit an inception of work report, progress reports, and a final report summarizing results achieved. In a surveying and mapping report, for example, the final report would include:

a. hard copies of satellite images used for the contract, geo-corrected and cut to sheet size;

b. computer tapes of all satellite images used for the contract in a format to be agreed on during the implementation phase of the contract;

c. graphical overlays of all map sheets with the extracted features on stable film; and

d. revision overlays of all map sheets on stable film, on which all detected changes are marked in different colors for different features.

Most of the projects executed by the United Nations and related agencies involve works designed to build the infrastructure or facilities of a member state. The government of the country involved usually agrees to provide to the contractor services and facilities such as basic background documentation, office space and secretarial services, and other items. The United Nations normally makes no representation that the full support and cooperation of the government will be ensured in the provision of personnel and facilities and assumes no responsibility for any delays or shortfalls that may result therefrom. The typical agreement does not relieve the contractor of its obligations under the contract due to delays or shortfalls caused by the government.

The price and payment terms section of the agreement sets the sum to be paid to the contractor and the modality of payment. A typical schedule of payments could be as follows:

a. immediately following the effective date of the contract, this initial payment to be made against a bank guarantee in terms acceptable to the UN to be issued at the instance of the contractor in favor of the UN by a reputable bank to guarantee faithful performance of the contractor's obligations under the contract. The guarantee is to remain in full force and effect from the effective date of the contract until the contractor has fulfilled all its obligations under the contract ending with the UN's acceptance of the final report referred to above. On receipt of the bank guarantee together with an original invoice the UN shall process the initial payment;
b. on receipt by the chief, Contracts and Procurement Service, of the first progress report certified for payment by the UN office concerned;
c. on receipt by the chief, Contracts and Procurement Service, of the second progress report certified for payment by the UN office concerned; and
d. on receipt by the chief, Contracts and Procurement Service, of the final report, together with all the required documents due under the contract, certified for payment by the UN office concerned.

Most types of procurement contracts entered into by the UN include a provision for the withholding of payments to the contractor. Such provisions grant the UN the right to withhold payment if the work under the contract is not performed to the reasonable satisfaction of the UN. The withholding by the UN of interim payments does not affect the contractor's obligation to continue performance under the contract pending resolution of the dispute pursuant to the general conditions. Also, the contractor is not entitled to interest on any late payment by the UN of sums payable under the contract.

As noted, the General Conditions for General Contracts of the United Nations are incorporated by reference in the specific agreements the organization enters into. They complete and integrate the specific contract provisions. They can be summarized as follows.

The legal status of a contractor vis-à-vis the United Nations is that of an independent contractor. The contractor's personnel and subcontractors are not considered in any respect as being the employees or agents of the United Nations. The contractor is responsible for the professional and technical competence of its employees and is required to select reliable individuals who will perform effectively in the implementation of the contract, respect the local customs, and conform to a high standard of moral and ethical conduct.

The contractor is not to assign, transfer, pledge, or make other disposition of the contract or any of the contractor's rights, claims, or obligations except with the prior written authorization of the United Nations. The United Nations further controls the contractor by requiring prior written approval and clearance of any subcontractors by the United Nations. The general conditions also forbid the contractor to seek or accept instructions from any authority external to the United Nations in connection with the performance of its services under a contract.

An important provision deals with indemnification. The contractor agrees to indemnify, hold and save harmless, and defend, at its own expense, the United Nations, its officials, agents, and employees from and against liability arising out of the acts or omissions of the contractor or its employees or subcontractors in the performance of the contract. The provision extends to claims and liability in the nature of workmen's compensation claims and those arising out of the use of patented inventions or devices.

The contractor is required to provide and maintain all appropriate workmen's compensation and liability insurance to cover its own employees and any claims for death, bodily injury, or damage to property arising out of the execution of the contract. Such liability insurance must include subcontractors. The contractor must not permit attachment or other encumbrance by any person to remain on file in any public office or on file with the United Nations against any monies due or to become due for any work done or materials furnished under the contract, or by reason of any other claim or demand against the contractor.

Title to any equipment and supplies that may be furnished by the United Nations rests with the organization and any such equipment must be returned to it at the conclusion of the contract or when no longer needed by the contractor. Obviously, the returned equipment must be in the same condition as when delivered to the contractor, subject to normal wear and tear.

The intellectual rights provision grants the United Nations the right to all patents, copyrights, and trademarks with regard to documents and other materials that bear a direct relation to the execution of the contract. At the request of the United Nations, the contractor must take all necessary steps, execute all necessary documents, and generally assist in securing such proprietary rights and transferring them to the United Nations in compliance with the requirements of applicable laws.

The general conditions of contract include a strict confidentiality provision. All maps, drawings, photographs, mosaics, plans, reports, recommendations, estimates, documents, and all other data compiled by or received by the contractor are the property of the United Nations; it must be treated as confidential and can only be released to the authorized UN officials on completion of work. The contractor may not communicate at any time to any other person, government, or external authority any information known to it by reason of its association with the United Nations that has not been made public except with the authorization of the United Nations. Such information cannot be used by the contractor for his private advantage. These obligations do not lapse on termination of the contract.

The force majeure and termination provisions are rather standard. The arbitration provision mandates the use of the United Nations Commission on International Trade Law (UNCITRAL) Arbitration Rules. For contracts within the United States arbitration is to be conducted under the auspices of the American Arbitration Association and for those outside the United States under the auspices of the International Chamber of Commerce, which must also serve as the appointing authority under the rules.

A special feature of the general conditions of contract is the section on privileges and immunities. According to Section 7 of the *Convention on Privileges and Immunities of the United Nations*, the UN and its subsidiary organs are exempt from all direct taxes and from customs duties in respect of articles imported or exported for its official use. The UN is therefore authorized to deduct from the contractor's invoice any amount representing such taxes or duties charged by the vendor to the United Nations. The contractor is to be wholly responsible for the payment, where payable, of all customs and other import duties.

OTHER UN-RELATED ORGANIZATIONS

The International Fund for Agricultural Development (IFAD) is an organization that may from time to time procure satellite services for the use of member states. We are going to look at the procurement procedures used by that organization as an example of what a contractor may expect in dealing with an international agency of this type. The following is a summary of the main provisions in the Procurement Guidelines of IFAD.

"International competitive bidding," as used in the guidelines, has the purpose of affording to prospective bidders from all member countries of the fund adequate notification of a recipient's requirements and providing all bidders an equal opportunity to bid on the necessary goods or works, subject to appropriate preferences for goods and services from developing member countries. In order to foster widespread competition, individual contracts must be of a size appropriate to attract bidders. The size and scope of individual contracts depend on the magnitude, nature, and location of the project.

Potential bidders are to be invited in a timely manner in order to be able to bid during the period established for that purpose. This is done by transmitting copies of the invitation to bid or the advertisement of the invitation to the fund and to local representatives of the eligible countries that are potential suppliers of the goods or services required. If an eligible country does not have a local representative, the invitation or advertisement for bidding must be sent to the government agency or other appropriate agency responsible for the foreign trade of such country. Invitations must also be published in the *Development Forum of the United Nations*, published by the Division for Economic and Social Information, and at least for four consecutive days in the recipient country's official newspaper or other publication of the widest possible circulation. In the event the recipient country does not have appropriate means to give proper publicity to an invitation to bid, it may request the fund to assist in arranging for such publicity. For large, specialized, or important contracts, the fund may, in addition, require that invitations to bid be advertised in well-known technical magazines, newspapers, and trade publications of wide international circulation in sufficient time before bids are to be opened to enable prospective bidders to request bidding documents and prepare bids.[3]

In order to ensure that invitations to bid are confined to capable firms, prequalification is advised for large or complex contracts. The financing agreement with the fund will specify whether prequalification is required with respect to particular contracts. Such a prequalification must be based entirely on the ability of the interested firm to perform the particular work under the contract in a satisfactory manner, taking into consideration, among other things, (a) experience and performance on contracts similar to those under the bid; (b) capabilities with respect to personnel, equipment, and plant; and (c) financial position. Prequalification must be advertised and notified as appropriate. The scope of work, abbreviated specifications, and a clear statement of the requirements for qualification must be sent to all firms desiring to be considered for prequalification.[4]

The bidding documents must furnish all information necessary to a bidder to prepare a tender for the goods and or services to be supplied. The documents may vary with respect to detail and complexity in accordance with the nature and size of the operations under the bid. Documents, however, must include the following: instructions to the tenderer; form of tender; form and conditions of contract, both general and special; technical and performance specifications; bill of quantities and drawings; and necessary appendices.

Invitations to bid must specify the period for which the bids remain valid. This period must be sufficient to enable the recipient to complete comparison and evaluation of bids and review the recommendation of award with the fund for approval so that the award can be notified within that period. Bid bonds or guarantees may be required, but they must not be set so high as to discourage suitable bidders from tendering.[5]

The contract documents must clearly define the scope of work to be performed or goods to be supplied, the rights and obligations of the recipient and of the contractor or manufacturer, and the powers and authority of the engineer or architect, if one is employed by the recipient, in the administration of the contract.[6]

Because most bids solicited by or on behalf of international agencies are invited from prospective bidders in a number of countries, it is necessary to make provision for pricing and currency of the bids. The IFAD Guidelines[7] require that bidding documents clearly state the currency or currencies in which bid prices are stated. Bidding documents should normally require the bidder to state the bid price, either in the bidder's own currency or in another currency widely used in international trade and specified in the bidding documents, except that

a. in contracts for the supply and installation of equipment, the bidding documents may specify that the bidder should state in the recipient's currency the portion of his bid price relating to the installation and
b. in the case of civil works, the bidding documents may require the bidder to state the bid's price entirely in the recipient's currency.

Payments under a contract should normally be made in the currency or currencies in which the price has been stated in the successful bid. However, the bid documents should always provide that, if the bidder expects to incur a portion of his expenditures in currencies other than those stated in his bid and so indicates in his bid, payment of the corresponding portion of the price so expended will be made in those currencies. Where a portion of the price under the contract is to be paid in a currency other than the currency of the bid, the contract must provide against a loss or gain to the contractor or supplier, as the case may be, from a variation in exchange rates between the currency of the bid and the other currency due or payable to the bidder under the contract. To that end, the contract must provide that amounts due or payable in a currency other than that of the bid shall be calculated at the rate of exchange between the two currencies specified for the purpose in the bidding documents.[8]

The guidelines do not specifically require that disputes be settled by arbitration but recommend arbitration over other dispute settlement mechanisms. Other provisions covered by the guidelines, such as liquidated damages and force majeure, are rather standard.

THE EUROPEAN SPACE AGENCY

In order to better understand the procurement practice of ESA, mention should be made of its general policy as laid down in its charter. Article II of the *ESA Convention* states as follows:

The purpose of the Agency shall be to provide for and to promote, for exclusively peaceful purposes, co-operation among European States in space research and technology and their space applications, with a view to their being used for scientific purposes and for operational space applications systems:

a. by elaborating and implementing a long-term European space policy, by recommending space objectives to the Member States, and by concerting the policies of the Member States with respect to other national and international organisations and institutions.
b. by elaborating and implementing activities and programmes in the space field.
c. by co-ordinating the European space programme and national programmes, and by integrating the latter progressively and as completely as possible into the European Space programme, and the development of application satellites.
d. by elaborating and implementing the industrial policy appropriate to its programme and by recommending a coherent industrial policy to the Member States.

The industrial policy mentioned in Article II is stated in more detail in Article VII:

The industrial policy which the Agency is to elaborate and apply by virtue of Article II d. shall be designed in particular to:

a. meet the requirements of the European space programme and the co-ordinated national space programmes in a cost-effective manner;

b. improve the world-wide competitiveness of European industry by maintaining and developing space technology and by encouraging the rationalization and development of an industrial structure appropriate to market requirements, making use in the first place of the existing industrial potential of all Member States;
c. ensure that all Member States participate in an equitable manner, having regard to their financial contribution, in implementing the European space programme and in the associated development of space technology; in particular the Agency shall, for the execution of its programmes, grant preference to the fullest extent possible to industry in all Member States, which shall be given the maximum opportunity to participate in the work of technological interest undertaken for the Agency;
d. exploit the advantages of competitive bidding in all cases, except where this would be incompatible with other defined objectives of industrial policy.

Annex V states in clear terms the preference it gives to European industry: "In the placing of contracts, the Agency shall give preference to industry and organisations of Member States."

The actual implementing rules for ESA procurement are set out in the *ESA Contracts Regulations*.[9] Article 5 of the Regulations provides that:

Open Competitive tender shall be the normal procedure for the placing of contracts. Restrictive competitive tender may be applied:

a. for supplies of services the special nature of which limits the capacity to provide them to few potential tenderers;
b. if the Industrial Policy Committee has given a directive or guideline to that effect to the Director General. Whenever possible, at least three potential tenderers shall nevertheless be invited to tender.

Noncompetitive tender is dealt with by Article 6 as follows:

1. Competitive tender may be waived only in the following cases:
   a. if only one source for the supplies and services exists;
   b. in the case of extreme operational urgency resulting from unforseeable events;
   c. where for scientific, technical or economic reasons contracts for additional or supplementary supplies or services cannot be separated from a previous contract;
   d. if the supplies or services required are the subject of intellectual property rights and can, as a consequence, only be procured from one particular source;
   e. if the expenditure involved does not exceed 100,000 Accounting Units; and
   f. if the Industrial Policy Committee has given a directive or a guideline to that effect to the director general.
2. Competitive tender may also be waived if, after Invitations to Tender have been issued, only one tender is admitted and a reissue of the Invitation to Tender

would be unlikely to obtain better results or would not be feasible due to extreme urgency.

According to an article by Stephen Kahn, head of Rules and Procedures of the ESA Contracts Department,[10] in spite of a businesslike and industrial orientation in ESA, some 70 percent of contracts are placed by direct negotiation. The major influence of industrial policy on contractor selection has apparently been far more in the choice of subcontractors for large projects. In the course of the last decade or so, projects have become fewer but larger and with a longer time span. Also, the number of potential prime contractors, that is, firms with sufficient size, system experience, and facilities, has been progressively reduced as a result of mergers.

In those cases where a particular state is funding a high proportion of a project because it or its industry has a particular interest in it, the prime contractor is basically already in place. ESA, however, follows a system of monitored competition for the subcontractors where the prime contractor is instructed to issue, for most subsystems, competitive invitations to tender.

The bid package in a tender consists of the following items:[11]

a. the cover letter, which lists the documents enclosed and states the closing date as well as any particular requirements of industrial policy;
b. the specifications required of the product and a work statement;
c. the draft contract, based on the General Conditions of Contract; and
d. the Special Conditions of Tender, which state how the bid is to be presented, and incorporate by reference the General Conditions of Tender.

The evaluation of bids is conducted by ESA under a set of procedures contained in the *Tender Evaluation Manual*. The basic principle is that a technical evaluation is made without any reference to the price. Only when the technical evaluation is complete are the offers ranked on the basis of technical quality and price. The final selection is made based on this ranking plus, where required, a consideration of the geographical location of the work offered. The evaluation is conducted by a Tender Evaluation Board whose independence is protected. For large projects, several evaluation panels covering the various areas are appointed.[12]

The policy of the European Space Agency with regard to the choice of law provisions in procurement contracts is to have each contract governed by the law of the contractor's place of business. The rationale behind that policy is that there would be no reason to insist on the law of ESA's headquarters or branches or any other specific law when dealing with customers from several countries. No specific law showed a particular advantage and there would be no sense in trying to force most contractors to do business under a foreign law.[13]

Disputes relating to ESA contracts are normally resolved through arbitration. If no other procedure is provided for under the contract, the rules of the International Chamber of Commerce apply, and arbitration will be held at a place close to the domicile of the contractors. It should be noted, however, that in spite of the large number of contracts placed, ESA has never had to go to arbitration.[14]

As we have seen for other international agencies, there is a significant question concerning pricing and currency exchanges. ESA's budget and internal accounting are carried out in Accounting Units, an artificial basket currency similar to the European currency unit (ECU). Member state contributions are assessed on the basis of gross national product using the Accounting Units and are paid to the agency in the national currency. The way ESA handles the currency problem of pricing is to break down prices and express them in the currency of each contractor, subcontractor, or subsubcontractor. In other words, the contract price is expressed in the currency of the country in which the work is to be executed. If the work is to be executed in several countries, the contract price may be split up into several currencies.[15]

Paragraphs 4 and 5 of Article 4 of the Contract Regulations describe the type of prices to be used in contracts as follows:

> 4. Contracts shall whenever possible be placed at fixed prices provided they are substantiated, by competition or otherwise, as being fair and reasonable. If a fixed price cannot be agreed prior to signature, the contract may be placed at a ceiling price to be converted into a fixed price as early as possible during the course of the contract. If a ceiling price cannot be agreed, the contract may be placed on a cost reimbursement basis. Incentives designed to achieve maximum economy and efficiency shall be included in contracts, where appropriate, particularly where they are to be placed on a cost-reimbursement basis.
> 5. Contracts at a ceiling price to be converted into a fixed price or on a cost-reimbursement basis shall be subject to cost control. In the case of contracts of major importance such control shall be undertaken during the execution of the contract.

The way ESA handles the problem of inflation in long-term projects is to include escalation clauses in contracts. An agreement will usually provide escalation formulas to apply to fixed prices and fixed price elements in an overall cost reimbursement price. In addition, ESA contracts apportion each price element according to the detailed breakdown given in the offer into its material and labor components. Appropriate indices relating to the relevant industry are then applied on a periodical basis to the amounts in question.[16]

Part II of the General Conditions for ESA Contracts contains some special conditions concerning intellectual property and associated rights for study and research and development contracts. As we see in the chapter on intellectual property, those provisions can acquire great importance in the context of a large project. Clause 37 provides, in part, as follows:

> The Contractor shall be the owner of any invention made in the course of or resulting from the work undertaken for the purpose of the contract and shall be entitled to protect such invention by patent or other form of industrial property right in accordance with applicable laws.
>
> In the event of a patent obtained by the Contractor in respect of any invention made in the course of or resulting from work undertaken for the purpose of the contract the Agency and the Member States (or Participating States) shall be entitled to a free of charge, non-exclusive, irrevocable license to use the invention for their own requirements in the field of space research and technology and their space applications and shall be allowed to grant sub-licenses for these purposes within the territory of the Member Sates (or Participating States). The Agency shall supply to the Contractor a list of the sub-licenses it has granted.

It is clear from this provision that the incentive of private companies to invest substantial funds in order to benefit from R&D activities is reduced by the limitations posed on the patents obtained. As commercial space develops further, particularly in the field of pharmaceuticals, there may be some modifications to the policy of ESA and other agencies with respect to patents.

In addition to the patent provisions, the General Conditions of Contract also deal with other types of intellectual property, such as copyright. Clause 38 provides in part as follows:

> Notwithstanding the copyright of the Contractor, and with due respect to the existence of any rights of third parties arising otherwise than from work performed for the purpose of the contract, the Agency and the Member States (or Participating States) shall be entitled to a free of charge, non-exclusive, irrevocable right to use, copy and disseminate the information for their own requirements in the field of space research and technology and their space applications.
>
> Information produced under the contract shall, consequently, not contain any copyright statements restricting the rights of the Agency or the Member States (or Participating States).
>
> The Contractor may, nevertheless, request the Agency to accept a more restrictive dissemination and use of the information than that to which it would be entitled by virtue of paragraph 1.3 above. The Agency has the right to refuse such request if the information concerned is the result of work performed for the purpose of the contract. If the information, however, is of a proprietary nature and not the result

of an Agency contract, or if the dissemination of the information would prejudice the justified interests of the Contractor, the Agency shall accept a restriction of the dissemination.

The same principles applying to patents and copyright are applied by ESA to the protection of computer software, namely, the contractor is entitled to enjoy legal protection with respect to computer software developed during the course of work under the contract, but the agency and member or participating states reserve the right to use and copy the software for their own requirements in the field of space research and technology.

The European Space Agency, pursuant to Clause 42 of the general conditions, restricts the transfer of technology and information to entities outside ESA and member states. Clause 42 specifically provides that any transfer by the Contractor to a non-member state or to an international organization, of inventions, information. or other assets of which he has acquired ownership by virtue of a contract with the agency, must respect the applicable export control laws and procedures in force in the state under whose jurisdiction the contractor is placed. Such transfers are furthermore subject to prior review by the agency and the member states. The review procedure is conducted under conditions of strict confidentiality.

NATIONAL GOVERNMENTS

The United Kingdom

In addition to participating in the programs of the European Space Agency, several member states undertake their own space projects. Some of those programs are related to defense activities as many countries increasingly view space activities such as remote sensing and satellite communications as critical to their defense needs. Also, departments of defense around the world have traditionally been powerful customers of aircraft manufacturers. Some of those manufacturers know that for both aircraft and spacecraft the government can be, and often is, the best customer. Particular attention should therefore be devoted to the procurement practices of some countries' defense departments.

Almost all UK defense procurement contracts are governed by the Standard Conditions of Government Contracts for Store Purchases.[17] Part I of those standard conditions deals with issues such as specifications, alteration of specifications, plans and drawings, inspection, and issues of government property as well as some labor related issues. It also makes reference, in Section 21, to the *Official Secrets Acts of 1911 to 1939*. That section requires the contractor to make sure that all persons employed on any work in connection with a contract have notice that the above statutory provisions apply to them and will continue to apply after the completion or earlier termination of the contract.

Part II of the standard conditions, among other things, deals with the applicable law, arbitration provisions, and intellectual rights issues. When the contract is made in England the applicable law is the English law and the Scots law in Scotland. For contracts made in England, disputes are to be submitted to arbitration of two persons, one to be appointed by the contractor and the other by the authority, or their umpire, in accordance with the provisions of the *Arbitration Act of 1950* and its amendments. In the case of Scottish contracts, disputes are also referred to the arbitration of two persons to be appointed by the authority and the contractor. In the case of difference of opinion between said persons, the dispute must be referred to an oversman who shall be chosen by the two arbitrators. The law of Scotland applies to both the arbitration and the enforcement of the award.

Under the provisions of Sections 55 and 56 of the *Patents Act of 1977*, and Section 12 of the *Registered Designs Act of 1949*, the contractor is authorized for the purpose of tendering for or performing under the contract to use any invention or design to which the said provisions relate and to use any model, document, or information relating to any such invention or design that may be required for that purpose. By Section 57 of the *Patents Act*, the contractor is released from liability under any license, assignment, assignation, or agreement to make any payments, whether by way of royalties, license fees, or similar expenses in respect of the contractor's use of any invention or design for the purpose of performing under the contract. Any expense relating to the mentioned royalties can be included by the contractor in or added to the contract price. These provisions flow from the contractor down to its subcontractors.

Section 59 of the standard conditions relates to security measures. A "secret matter" is defined as "any matter connected with or arising out of the execution of the contract or the work to be carried out thereunder which has been, or may hereafter be, by a notice in writing given by the Authority to the contractor, designated 'top secret,', 'secret' or 'confidential.' " References to a person employed by the contractor include "any person employed or engaged by the contractor to do anything in connection with the contract, whether under a contract of service with the contractor or under any other contract or arrangement whatsoever."

Paragraph 2 of Section 59 provides as follows:

The Contractor shall not, either before or after the completion or determination of the Contract, do or permit to be done anything which he knows or ought reasonably to know may result in information about a secret matter being:—

a. without the prior consent in writing of the Authority, disclosed to or acquired by any person who is an alien or who is a British subject by virtue only of a certificate of naturalization in which his name was included;
b. disclosed to or acquired by a person as respects whom the Authority has given to the Contractor a notice in writing which has not been canceled stating that the Authority requires that secret matters shall not be disclosed to that person;
c. without the prior consent of the Authority, disclosed to or acquired by any person who is not a servant of the Contractor;
d. disclosed to or acquired by a person who is a servant of the Contractor except in a case where it is necessary for the proper performance of the Contract that person shall have that information.

In some cases, these security provisions also extend to parties other than the contractor. The contractor is required to place every person employed by him (other than a subcontractor for the carrying out of anything to be done under the contract) who in his opinion has or will have such knowledge of any secret matter as to appreciate its significance under a duty to the contractor to observe the same obligations in relation to that matter as are imposed on the contractor. Before entering into any subcontract, where the work to be performed includes or will involve disclosure of information about a secret matter, the contractor is required to refer to the authority for approval a statement of the work to be carried out under that subcontract and the name and other particulars of the proposed subcontractor.

The United States

The United States is and has always been at the forefront of most space science and activities. Until recently, the major American aerospace companies had very little competition from foreign firms and their economic prosperity and growth seemed unstoppable. The reason for the rapid expansion of the aerospace industry has been the enormous amount of capital that the U.S. Defense Department and related agencies have poured on aerospace contractors. Although technically not a subsidy, the heavy defense investment in the industry has given it a boost that would have never been possible through the market forces alone. American contractors know, therefore, that their best, and sometimes only customer, is the U.S. government. For that reason, the highly developed federal procurement system is a subject of great interest to any company directly or indirectly involved with space and related activities.

It is outside the scope of this book to try to describe all the procurement laws and regulations which govern contracts with the U.S. government. Some observations, however, are offered to give a sense of how the system works and how procurement for space and related products and services may be different from other types of government acquisition.

The System of Federal Acquisition Regulations was established for the codification and publication of uniform policies and procedures for acquisition by all executive agencies. The System consists of the *Federal Acquisition Regulations* (FAR), which is the primary document, and agency acquisition regulations that implement or supplement the FAR. The FAR system does not include internal agency guidance procedures,[18] which are regulated by Section 48 of the *Code of Federal Regulations.*[19] That section provides that an agency head may issue or authorize the issuance of agency acquisition regulations that implement or supplement the FAR and incorporate, together with the FAR, agency policies, procedures, contract clauses, solicitation provisions, and forms that govern the contracting process or otherwise control the relationship between the agency, including any of its suborganizations and contractors or prospective contractors. An agency head may issue or authorize the issuance of internal agency guidance at any organizational level.

Pursuant to the *Office of Federal Procurement Policy Act*, as amended,[20] and other applicable statutes, when agency acquisition regulations have a significant effect beyond the internal operating procedures of the agency or have a significant cost or administrative impact on contractors or offerors, they must be published for comment in the *Federal Register*. Agency acquisition regulations implementing or supplementing the FAR have been enacted for:

1. the military departments and defense agencies, issued subject to the authority of the secretary of defense;
2. NASA activities, issued subject to the authorities of the administrator of NASA; and
3. the civilian agencies other than NASA, issued by the heads of those agencies subject to the overall authority of the administrator of general services or independent authority the agency may have.

Subchapter F of Section 32 of the *Code of Federal Regulations* governs the Defense Acquisition Regulatory System. The provisions in that section apply to the Office of the Secretary of Defense, the Organization of the Joint Chiefs of Staff, the military departments, and the defense agencies. The provisions also apply to other federal agencies that are directed by the Office of Federal Procurement Policy, Office of Management and Budget, to comply with those provisions. The Defense Acquisition Regulatory System (DARS) is defined by the regulations as "a system of policies and regulations to guide managers in the conduct of DoD acquisition activities and also to provide the detailed functional regulations required to govern DoD contractual actions in accordance with applicable laws and the need for efficiency."[21]

The *Defense Acquisition Regulation* (DAR) replaces the *Armed Services Procurement Regulation* (ASPR), and all laws, policies, and procedures applicable to the ASPR are equally applicable to the DAR. The Defense Acquisition Regulatory Council (DARC) is in charge of supporting the council director in the management of the DARS and in the development and implementation of required policy and procedures. The DARC membership includes a policy and a legal representative from each of the military departments and from the Defense Logistics Agency.

Substantive changes to DARS policy and procedures can be proposed by submitting appropriate recommendations to include specific regulatory language to the director of contract and system acquisition. It is interesting to note that changes may not only be proposed by DoD organizations and other federal agencies, but also by the private sector. Private sector entities with an interest in DARS policy can submit proposed changes directly. Industry associations may designate an individual to the council director and establish procedures for the individual to represent the association in commenting on DARS policy actions prior to final action by the council.

The U.S. Air Force. A good example of U.S. government procurement, and one that is very important to aerospace contractors, are the regulations for acquisition by the Air Force. As was mentioned above, the Air Force Supplement (AFFARS or AFFAR Supplement) to the *Federal Acquisition Regulation* and *DoD FAR Supplement* (DFARS) is issued under statutory authority of the secretary of defense and by order of the secretary of the Air Force. The AFFARS contains material that implements the FAR and DFARS and also contains supplementary material that is unique to the Department of the Air Force. The supplement, however, is not a stand-alone document but must be read in conjunction with the FAR and DFARS. Following is a general description of the main issues dealt with by those regulations.

Part 5301 of the regulations describes the Federal Acquisition Regulations System as it applies to the Air Force. The items covered under that part include the deviations from the FAR, agency, and public participation, contracting authority and responsibilities, and the clearance process.

Of particular interest to the prospective contractor is the clearance process whose objectives are designed to ensure that:

a. solicitations effectively implement approved acquisition strategies;
b. negotiation objectives represent fair and reasonable business arrangements and are consistent with law and regulation;
c. negotiated business arrangements, including pricing and other contractual terms and conditions, achieve agreed on objectives;
d. contracts clearly reflect the complete agreement of the parties and are consistent with laws, regulations and policies; and
e. the Air Force management is provided feedback on the operation of its contracting system, implementation of contracting policies, and the quality of contract actions, allowing management to foster continuous process improvement.[22]

The part further defines the terms "contract clearance," "business clearance," "competitive acquisition," "noncompetitive acquisition," and others. It also specifies the roles and responsibilities of the service acquisition executive, the deputy assistant secretary, the contracting officer, and other authorities and major commands.[23]

The Request for Business Clearance must be accompanied by the following documents:

1. the Request for Proposals;
2. the Preliminary Price Negotiation Memorandum, prepared in accordance with the FAR, to the extent that the required information is available prior to beginning negotiations;
3. the proposed request for Best and Final Offer, including the cover letter, the proposed contract, and any other attachments referred to in the cover letter;
4. determination of adequate price competition;
5. the official contract file, which must include technical evaluations, evidence of legal review, audit reports and any other field pricing reports; and
6. the offeror's proposal.

The contracting officer prepares a Request for Business Clearance (RBC) by requesting approval to proceed to award without discussions or requesting Best and Final Offers. In noncompetitive acquisitions, the Request for Business Clearance constitutes the contracting officer's request for approval of negotiation objectives and authority to begin negotiations with the contractor. If a business clearance document states conditions, the AFFARS provide that the contracting officer must not proceed with the requested action until all conditions have been met. The contracting officer must document in the contract file the specific actions taken to satisfy each condition.

In noncompetitive acquisitions, no further communications with the business clearance reviewing and approving authorities is required, unless there is a need for a substantial change from the approved clearance. Examples of changes that would require approval, include (a) a change in contract type, (b) a major change in the quantity or the nature of what the government is buying, and (c) a major change of a contract term or condition if that term or condition was considered critical by the Business Clearance Authority when the RBC was approved.

The Request for Contract Clearance must be accompanied by the following documents:

1. the negotiated contract document, bearing the contractor's signature and otherwise ready for signature by the contracting officer;
2. the final Price Negotiation Memorandum, which must incorporate the unchanged preliminary memorandum that accurately describes the proposed and objective positions as of the time of the business clearance; and
3. the official contract file. In noncompetitive actions for which the contract clearance approving authority was the business clearance reviewing authority, the contracting officer may provide an abbreviated file containing only the following documents:
   i. the Certificate of Current Cost or Pricing Data;
   ii a copy of each audit or field pricing report not included or considered in the Request for Business Clearance;
   iii. funding documents;
   iv. legal review; and
   v. the Individual Procurement Action Report.

Contract clearance is not required for competitive acquisitions unless specifically requested by the contracting officer or directed by the contract clearance approving authority. Reasons for requesting or directing a contract clearance may include:

1. when expected adequate price competition was not realized;
2. when significant issues remained unresolved after receipt and evaluation of the Best and Final Offer;
3. when one or more offerors introduced some significant change in the Best and Final Offer; or

4. when there are concerns about procurement integrity matters or a potential for debarment or suspension of an involved offeror.

Part 5304 of the regulations deals with administration matters, including contract execution, reporting, files, and the safeguarding of classified information within the industry. Part 5306 lists competition requirements. It defines "commencement of negotiations" as follows:

a. for noncompetitive negotiations, the acquisition cycle may proceed up to, but not including, the start of discussions with offerors for the purpose of reaching agreement on all aspects of the proposal, including terms and conditions and the pricing arrangement.
   b. For competitive negotiations, the acquisition cycle may proceed up to, but not including, competitive range determination if the competitive range determination will result in the elimination of an offeror; and may otherwise proceed up to, but not including, issuing the request for Best and Final Offer (BAFO).

Part 5307 of the regulations deals with acquisition planning. Part 5308 lists some required sources of acquisition supplies, such as the blind and other severely handicapped. Contractor qualification requirements are contained in Part 5309. When there may be some question about the ability of the prospective contractor to adequately perform, appropriate technical personnel from the concerned installation must participate in a preaward survey. Areas of interest might include performance plans, quality controls, personnel recruitment and training, work load factors for manpower utilization, handling or providing equipment, and any other area having a significant bearing on the contractor's ability to perform. Particular care is to be exercised in situations where the low responsive bidder has a bid price significantly below other bidders or the government estimate.

Provision is made for the debarment, suspension, and ineligibility of contractors. The Air Force Debarment and Suspension Review Board reviews recommendations from Air Force field activities regarding potential debarment or suspension of contractors and individuals. Ineligible parties are listed in the General Services Administration (GSA) List of Parties Excluded from Federal Procurement and Non-Procurement Programs. In special circumstances, a contracting officer can prepare a request for an exception with complete and detailed information relative to the contemplated procurement action. Such information should include all efforts taken to establish alternate sources and the impact to the Air Force if approval is not granted.

Part 5314 of the regulations deals with sealed bidding, whereas Part 5315 provides guidelines for contracting by negotiation. Special provision is made for the handling of responses received as a result of a notice of proposed sole source contract action. The contracting officer must transmit the respondent's information to the technical personnel and request a written technical assessment. The technical assessment and other relevant information must be used by the contracting officer to evaluate the response. Factors to be considered are the acquisition history, availability of reprocurement data, and contractor capabilities.

Subpart 5315.8 of the regulations, which deals with price negotiation, provides for a waiver of the requirement of the contractor to submit cost or pricing data. It also describes the price analysis and review technique for spares/support equipment (PARTS). PARTS is a pricing technique that provides for review of each line item in a spare parts or support equipment price proposal. When a proposal contains multiple line items, and the contracting officer determines that a detailed analysis of each line item is impractical, the proposal is evaluated as follows:

1. a detailed cost analysis is performed on
   a. those items where the proposed unit price exceeds 25 percent of the lowest unit price paid for the item at any time within the past twelve month period. The proposed prices of all items are compared to previous prices paid for that item.
   b. high value items representing a significant portion of the total proposal value;
2. those items not subjected to a detailed cost analysis are subjected to a value review to determine if their prices appear to be fair and reasonable (this review involves a subjective assessment of each line item);
3. A random sample of those items that, on first appearance, are determined to have an apparent fair and reasonable value, is selected for a detailed cost analysis by means of a random number tables or computer selection routines; and
4. the combination of the analysis efforts described, plus other appropriate inputs, are used to establish the government negotiation position for all line item prices, as well as for total price.

Parts 5316 and 5317 of the regulations deal with various types of contracts, such as fixed price and incentive contracts, and with special contracting methods, whereas Part 5319 states Air Force policy regarding small business and small disadvantaged business concerns. Foreign acquisition provisions are contained in Part 5325, and they define the format for nonavailability determination as well as international agreements and coordination.

Contract termination, both for convenience and for default, is governed by regulations Part 5349. An important provision deals with the termination of cost reimbursement contracts. The standard termination clause for that type of contract provides that the contracting officer and the contractor negotiate the settlement of the fee. Any method that is fair and equitable to both parties can be used. When the parties are unable to agree on the adjustment, the percentage of completion formula contained in the contract clause should be used. One method of estimating the percentage of completion is to compare the actual costs incurred with the estimated cost to complete the contract, adjusting the resulting percentage according to the difficulty or importance of each type of cost. Under this method, the contracting officer should prepare a breakdown of the estimated costs negotiated in connection with awarding the contract and an estimate of the cost to complete each category of items as shown in the contractor's settlement proposal. In determining the extent of completion, each category of work accomplished is separately evaluated, giving greater weight to those elements that reflect the most substantial or significant work.

The U.S. Navy. The U.S. Navy is a good customer of major aerospace contractors, particularly in the field of satellites. Following is a brief mention of some of the provisions that govern acquisition procedures.

The *Navy Acquisition Procedures Supplement* (NAPS) implements and supplements the *Federal Acquisition Regulation* and the *Department of Defense FAR Supplement*. It establishes uniform policies and procedures to be followed by all Department of the Navy contracting personnel in acquiring required supplies and services. As in the Air Force regulations, the NAPS is not intended to be a stand-alone document and must be read in consonance with the FAR and DFARS.

As in other federal procurement practice, before entering into a contract, the government has to meet certain requirements. A basic requirement is the business clearance. Its purpose is to demonstrate that the proposed acquisition conforms to good business practices and Navy acquisition policies. Additionally, the business clearance serves as the historical record of the business/pricing aspects of an acquisition and justifies, by written evidence, that the price established is fair and reasonable. Consequently, the business clearance must show all significant facts considered in reaching agreement as well as how the facts presented influenced estimated cost judgments. For competitive negotiated acquisitions the business clearance serves as the historical record of the source selection process where factors in addition to price may serve as the primary basis for award. Each acquisition must be supported by both a prenegotiation and postnegotiation business clearance.[24]

In single source acquisitions, the purpose of the prenegotiation business clearance is to set forth all significant details of the proposed contract negotiation and the course to be pursued. In addition, the prenegotiation business clearance should document how the contractor developed its proposal position, what the field price analyst/technical/auditor did to develop their recommended positions and how the negotiator developed the prenegotiation position. Finally, the prenegotiation clearance should demonstrate that the negotiator is adequately prepared to enter negotiations, that adequate facts have been obtained, that these facts have been evaluated and that the judgments made in arriving at the prenegotiation objective are sound.

The purpose of the postnegotiation business clearance is to demonstrate that the business/pricing agreement reached is a fair and reasonable one and to complete the historical record concerning the acquisition initiated in the prenegotiation business clearance. The postnegotiation clearance must complement the cost and price analysis by presenting additional facts obtained during negotiation that affected the judgments made in the previous clearance and must justify differences between the prenegotiation business clearance objective and the negotiated settlement.

In competitive acquisitions, the prenegotiation business clearance documents the technical and cost/price evaluation, the basis for determining the competitive range, and the areas for discussions with offerors determined to be within the competitive range. Competitive range determinations may be presented in the prenegotiation business clearance or in a separate business clearance for competitive range only. The postnegotiation business clearance documents the events leading to the request and receipt of the best and final offers, the technical and cost/price evaluation thereof, the rationale supporting the source selection decision and the determination that the award price is fair and reasonable. In individual cases, a waiver of the postnegotiation business clearance may be requested from the approval authority. If a waiver is granted, a brief memorandum for the record must be prepared to address compliance with the limitations prescribed in the waiver, document the results of the negotiation, and address the postnegotiation clearance compliances.

Prenegotiation and postnegotiation business clearances, among other situations, must be prepared and approved for the following contract actions:

1. negotiated contracts or contract modifications for the acquisition of supplies or services not within the scope or under the terms of an existing contract;
2. competitive range determinations;
3. basic ordering agreements;

4. modifications and changes issued pursuant to contract clauses such as those entitled "changes," or "government property";
5. exercise or pricing of an unpriced base allocation option; and
6. retroactive price redetermination after completion.

Part 5207 of NAPS governs acquisition planning. It requires written acquisition plans to be prepared for all acquisitions involving the development, production or support of weapons systems, subsystems, or certain types of equipment. Examples of program-based acquisition plans include aircraft; helicopters; drones and targets; missiles; launchers; tracked and wheeled vehicles; guided munitions; bombs; guns; mines; torpedoes; radars; surveillance, command, control, and communication; electronic warfare; propulsion; astronautics and spacecraft; telemetry; photographic and meteorological equipment; and tactical computers and associated software. Acquisition plans must be approved by the appropriate executive officers, direct reporting program managers, or their designees. For all acquisition category programs, an Acquisition Strategy Report must be approved by the Milestone Decision Authority in advance of any acquisition plan approval.

Part 5209 of NAPS deals with contractor qualifications. The adequacy of a contractor's past performance is considered a major factor in determining responsibility. When little or no contractor performance data is available within the contracting office, the cognizant contract administration should be asked to assess the prospective contractor's ability to meet contract requirements and request a preaward survey encompassing an evaluation of the adequacy of the contractor's quality control system. Performance data may include the following:

a. acquisition history, such as records of previous contract performance, outstanding claims, termination for default, and the like;
b. contractor plant visits;
c. product deficiency reporting and feedback; and
d. waiver/deviation requests, frequency, and repetitiveness.

Part 5214 of the regulations deals with bids and contract awards, whereas Part 5215 governs contracting by negotiation, including source selection and evaluation factors. "Best value" is defined as the evaluation of proposals and selection of a source based on cost/price, and other evaluation factors, such as technical competence, proven past performance, management capability, life cycle costs, and quality. Best value evaluations are to be employed whenever possible and especially in weapons systems and professional and technical services support acquisitions. Requirements that dictate complex integration of people, equipment, hardware, innovation, and software should also be evaluated on a best value basis.

As part of the proposal analysis, the NAPS refer to the cost realism analysis. That type of analysis involves a summary level review of the cost portion (excluding profit/fee) of the offerors' proposals to determine if the overall costs proposed are realistic for the work to be performed. Cost realism analysis differs from the detailed cost analysis usually undertaken in a noncompetitive procurement to determine the reasonableness of the various cost elements and profit/fee to arrive at a fair and reasonable price.

One of the factors involved in a proposal analysis are subcontract pricing considerations. The need for requiring submission by potential and existing contractors of information regarding the purchased materials portion of price quotations is emphasized by the NAPS. This information is deemed necessary particularly when competition is lacking or is inadequate to control the prices initially proposed. The prime categories requiring subcontract information are new contracts in cases involving a sole source or where competition is limited. The type of information required in a proposal would include:

a. principal materials or components to be purchased,
b. proposed or established sources,
c. proposed method of purchase,
d. basis for award,
e. copies of suppliers' cost breakdown and any price analysis made by the contractor, and
f. type of pricing arrangement.

Important insurance provisions are contained in Part 5228 of NAPS, summarized as follows. The policy of the Department of the Navy (DoN) is to rely on the commercial insurance industry to the maximum extent practicable to protect contractors against risks arising under contracts. In some situations, however, it may be preferable or necessary to provide government indemnification when, for instance,

a. there is a continuing program, such as for nuclear vessels, and insurance premiums costs over a period of time could equal the amount of coverage;
b. there is a war risk in areas where hostilities are involved;
c. the cost of insurance is so excessive that it is unreasonable;

d. the government risk is rated only on its isolated experience and not shared with the risk of others;

e. an urgent requirement does not allow sufficient time to receive a competitive insurance quotation;

f. the degree of risk is either very small or catastrophic; or

g. the indemnification of the deductible portion of insurance coverage will substantially reduce insurance costs.

Protests, disputes, and appeals procedures are contained in Part 5233 of NAPS and basically reiterate the basic principles of federal procurement. The general approach is to conduct acquisition programs in a manner calculated to minimize the occurrence of claims by the contractor. The causes of claims are to be minimized through realistic planning and contracting, careful attention to the action required to meet the DoN's obligations and tight control over the changes process. Other provisions state the procedure for claims reporting, review, and approval requirements.

The U.S. Defense Agencies. A good example of the procurement practice of defense agencies is given by the *Defense Mapping Agency Federal Acquisition Regulation* (MFARS), which implements and/or supplements FAR and the *Department of Defense FAR Supplement.*

The DMA Deputy director, management and technology, is designated acting DMA senior procurement executive and authorized to perform the duties of the position in the absence of the DMA senior procurement executive when delay in any action would result in adverse impact to the DMA mission. The DMA chief of staff is the DMA competition advocate.

In addition to the review and approval required for certain contracting actions by the director of acquisitions, it is DMA policy that agency legal counsel participate fully in the entire acquisition process and that contracting personnel seek legal advice and assistance from counsel during all phases of the acquisition process.

Part 5 of the regulations details the requirements for publicizing contract actions, whereas Part 6 deals with competition requirements, including justification and approval for other than full and open competition. Part 7 governs acquisition planning and it incorporates by reference the principles of acquisition planning set forth in FAR and DFAR. It also requires the contracting officer preparing the acquisition plan to enlist the aid of cognizant engineering, technical, production, logistics, quality assurance, maintenance, and comptroller personnel in order to provide the information required by the regulations.

The acquisition plan for a purchase request must include certain information. It must describe the need for the purchase as well as the required capabilities or performance characteristics of the supplies or services being acquired. It should discuss the technical history and program background of the acquisition, providing information on previous acquisitions for the same or similar supplies or service. Cost goals must be stated for the acquisition and the rationale supporting them, including the cost concepts to be employed. Delivery or performance-period requirements should be described. A description must be included on the competition, that is, how it is sought, promoted, and sustained throughout the course of the acquisition. The method of source selection must also be discussed; for instance, price or technical competition, formal source selection, including the timing for submission and evaluation of proposals. Contracting considerations should be stated. They include contract type selection, options, level of quality program, special contracting methods, any special contract clauses, solicitations provisions, FAR/DFARS/MFARS deviations required, and any other special considerations. Logistics considerations should also be included in the plan.

Part 9 of the MFARS governs issues related to contractor qualifications. Part 14 deals with sealed bidding, including opening of bids and award of contract. Part 15 governs the contracting by negotiation. In that area, it should be noted that DMA's policy is to encourage submission of unsolicited research proposals and avoid organizational or regulatory constraints that may inhibit generation and acceptance of innovative and unique research ideas from prospective contractors.

In the context of source selection, Subpart 5.6 defines greatest value score evaluations as a specific contracting technique that may be used for competitive negotiated acquisitions when it is determined necessary to award the contract to the offeror that receives the highest weighted score resulting from evaluation of a combination of price and nonprice factors. This technique is applicable and may be used when the following elements are present:

1. the requirement must be suitable for a firm fixed price type or contract;
2. evaluation of proposals elements other than price, that is, technical and management, is required;
3. the nonprice elements lend themselves to the development of meaningful standards against which the proposals may be evaluated;
4. the procurement does not warrant a formalized source selection organizational structure with a source selection authority, boards, and committees; and,
5. detailed cost analysis to determine cost completeness, realism, and reasonableness is not required.

When using the greatest value score technique, contracting and technical personnel must agree on the relative weight of price considerations versus considerations other than price. The evaluation must use weights. Price must carry a weight of at least 20 percent, and the total nonprice factors may total a weight of no more than 80 percent. The evaluation plan must describe each factor being evaluated, the total number of points available for each factor, and how those points are to be assigned. Examples of nonprice factors include technical areas, such as past experience in the cartographic discipline, production processes and quality, and management items, such as organization and training.

Part 15.612–90 describes the policy for formal source selection within the DMA. Source selection procedures are designed to ensure impartial and comprehensive evaluation of competitive technical proposals, which should result in the selection of a source whose performance is expected to best meet the agency's objectives at an affordable cost. One of the precautions adopted to meet these criteria is to avoid contacts between prospective contractors and senior agency personnel after the source selection is under way. The formal source selection process is not intended for broad and indiscriminate use. It is an administratively costly acquisition method and should apply only to complex requirements that warrant the use of the time and resources.

The referred to formal source selection process contemplates the creation of a separate source selection organization. All persons involved in the source selection process (including people other than DMA personnel) must inform the Source Selection Evaluation Group chairperson if their participation in source selection activities might result in a real, apparent, or possible conflict of interest. Such people may have to be disqualified. A successful source selection requires close coordination among the people involved in it. The following responsibilities and duties serve to maintain an effective check and balance system during the process:

1. The project manager and the contracting officer have joint responsibility for preparation of the acquisition plan and the source selection plan.
2. The requirements office must prepare a complete purchase request package, including Statement of Work, schedules, specifications, and the like, required to develop an adequate solicitation.
3. The project manager and the contracting office must jointly develop/establish the source list and prepare a synopsis and transmit it to the Commerce Business Daily.
4. The contracting officer is responsible for conducting preproposal briefings, debriefing unsuccessful offerors, making competitive range determinations,

establishing procedures to protect contractor proposal information and government source selection data, and determining contractor responsibility. The contract team is responsible for preparing the solicitation and is in charge of all contract negotiations. The leader of the technical evaluation team selects the evaluators and ensures that the relative order of importance of the criteria is established and provided to the contract team to be included in the solicitation. The technical evaluation team establishes the basis for the technical evaluation of the proposals, develops the evaluation criteria and standards, and rates the technical elements of the proposals. The chairperson of the Source Selection Evaluation Team, together with the contracting officer and the technical evaluation team leader, analyzes the individual proposal evaluation summaries and prepares the proposal analysis report, which summarizes the resultant ranking of each technical proposal. At the end of the process, the source selection decision document is signed by the source selection authority, and forwarded to the contracting officer who executes the contract.

Part 25 of the MFARS governs foreign acquisitions and Part 27 patents, data, and copyrights only adding details, however, to the regulations it supplements. Part 32 deals with contract financing. Part 33 governs protests, disputes, and appeals. It describes the procedure and the practical approach of the agency when the protest is lodged with the agency and when it is lodged with the General Accounting Office or other authority.

Part 42 of the MFARS govern contract administration and postaward orientation. Due to the specialized nature of the DMA's products and services, the skills and resources of the agency are provided to assist contract administration/audit performed by Department of Defense agencies on DMA requirements. Part 49 deals with contract termination and specifically sets out the procedure for termination for default.

National Aeronautics and Space Administration. NASA's Supplement to the Federal Acquisition Regulations is somewhat comprehensive but straightforward. As an example of NASA's procurement practice, we examine some provisions of a sample Request for Proposal (RFP) for a hardware type of contract.[25] Although the provisions discussed below are not universal, they can be considered standard for that type of acquisition.

The section on the scope of work provides that the contractor supply the personnel, materials, and facilities necessary to design, develop, and test the user transponders subject of the contract. The contractor is to submit separate monthly progress reports on all work accomplished during each month of contract performance. The report must be a summary presentation of the progress, problem areas, activities on-going and planned, including status of procurements, personnel changes, and must include the performance assurance status reports.

The contract must specify the location for acceptance, in this case the Goddard Space Flight Center. If it is a fixed price contract, acceptance is deemed to have occurred constructively—for the sole purpose of computing an interest penalty that might be due the contractor under the *Prompt Payment Act* —on the seventh day after the contractor has delivered the supplies or services in accordance with the terms and conditions of the contract. In the event that actual acceptance occurs within the constructive acceptance period, the determination of an interest penalty is to be based on the date of the actual acceptance. At the time of each delivery, the contractor must furnish to the government a Material Inspection and Receiving Report.

The contractor is required to provide and maintain an inspection system acceptable to the government covering the work under this contract. The government has the right to inspect and test all work called for by the contract, to the extent practicable at all places and times, including the period of performance, and in any event before acceptance. The government may also inspect the premises of the contractor or any subcontractor involved. If the government performs any inspection or test on the premises of the contractor or a subcontractor, the contractor must furnish and require subcontractors to furnish all reasonable facilities and assistance for the safe and convenient performance of these duties. The government will normally bear the expense of government inspections or tests made at other than the contractor's or subcontractor's premises. The government must accept or reject the work as promptly as practicable after delivery. Government failure to inspect and accept or reject the work does not relieve the contractor from responsibility, nor impose liability on the government, for nonconforming work. Work is nonconforming when it is defective in material or workmanship or is otherwise not in conformity with contract requirements. The government has the right to reject nonconforming work. If the contractor fails or is unable to correct or to replace nonconforming work within the delivery schedule, the contracting officer may accept the work and make an equitable price reduction. Failure to agree on a price reduction constitutes a dispute. Inspection and test by the government does not relieve the contractor from responsibility for defects or other failures to meet the contract requirements that may be discovered before acceptance. Acceptance is conclusive, except for latent defects, fraud, gross mistakes amounting to fraud, or as otherwise specified in the contract.

Title to supplies furnished under the contract passes to the government on formal acceptance, regardless of when or where the government takes physical possession, unless the contract specifically provides for earlier passage of title. Unless the contract specifically provides otherwise, risk of loss or damage to supplies remains with the contractor until:

1. delivery of the supplies to a carrier, if transportation is f.o.b. origin, or
2. acceptance by the government or delivery of the supplies to the government at the destination specified in the contract, whichever is later, if transportation is f.o.b. destination.

This provision does not apply to supplies that so fail to conform to contract requirements as to give a right of rejection. The risk of loss of or damage to such nonconforming supplies remains with the contractor until cure or acceptance. Also, the contractor is not liable for loss of or damage caused by the negligence of officers, agents, or employees of the government acting within the scope of their employment.

A clause on liquidated damages may provide that if the contractor fails to deliver the supplies within the time specified, he shall, in place of actual damages, pay to the government as fixed, agreed, and liquidated damages, a specified sum for each calendar day of delay. Alternatively, if delivery or performance is so delayed, the government may terminate the contract in whole or in part and, in that event, the contractor is liable for fixed, agreed, and liquidated damages accruing until the time the government may reasonably obtain delivery or performance of similar supplies or services. The liquidated damages are in addition to excess costs under the termination clause. The contractor, however, is not charged with liquidated damages when the delay in delivery or performance arises out of causes beyond the control and without the fault or negligence of the contractor.

A stop-work clause may provide that the contracting officer may, at any time, by written order to the contractor, require the contractor to stop all, or any part, of the work called for by this contract for a specified period after the order is delivered to the contractor, and for any further period to which the parties may agree. On receipt of such an order, the contractor must immediately comply with its terms and take all reasonable steps to minimize the incurrence of costs allocable to the work covered by the order during the period of work stoppage. Within the stoppage period the contracting officer must either cancel the stop-work order or terminate the work covered by the order according to the termination provisions. If a stop-work order is canceled or the period of the order expires, the contractor must resume work. The contracting officer will then make an equitable adjustment in the delivery schedule or contract price, or both.

If the performance of all or part of the work under a contract is delayed or interrupted by an unauthorized act or omission of the contracting officer, an adjustment must be made for any increase in the cost of performance of the contract caused by the delay or interruption and the contract must be modified in writing accordingly. Adjustment must also be made in the delivery dates and any other contractual term affected by the delay. However, no adjustment is to be made if performance would have been delayed or interrupted by any other cause including the fault or negligence of the contractor.

An important section of the solicitation describes the evaluation factors for award. They are mission suitability, cost/price, relevant experience, and past performance, and other considerations.

The mission suitability evaluation factor indicates, for each offeror, the merit or excellence of the work to be performed or work to be delivered. It includes, as appropriate, both technical and management subfactors. Because this factor can be highly technical and must be integrated in order to convey an overall evaluation of relative merit, mission suitability and its supporting factors are numerically weighted and scored. The cost/price evaluation factor is used to assess what each offeror's proposal will probably cost the government if selected. Proposed costs are analyzed to determine the probable "cost of doing business" based on the offeror's proposed approach. Further, this analysis identifies and assesses the impact of features that cause a proposal to cost more or less than other proposals. The relevant experience and past performance evaluation factor indicates the relevant quantitative and qualitative aspects of each offeror's record of performing services or delivering products similar in type, size, and complexity to the requirements of the solicitation. This factor provides an opportunity to evaluate the quality of goods and services provided by the offerors to the agency and other government organizations as either a prime or subcontractor.

The mission suitability evaluation factor includes several subfactors under which there may be one or more elements. They can be summarized as follows:

1. Technical Approach. The proposal is evaluated to determine the proposer's understanding of the hardware application to the mission, as well as methods proposed to meet mission requirements. The mechanical design approach is to be evaluated in terms of construction, layout, modularity, weight requirements, and electronics. The electronics approach is to be evaluated for conformance to accepted space electronics design practices that include both adequate design and high power efficiency. The use of space-qualified and currently available electronics components and parts will be evaluated, especially with respect to the specified radiation environment. The thermal design approach will be reviewed for its ability to provide adequate temperature margins for performance and parts reliability. The proposed systems design is also evaluated for its overall

performance in relation to the mission, its lack of unnecessary complexity, and its interfaces to the spacecraft systems.

2. Program Management. The government evaluates the contractor's plans to organize and effectively manage and control all the necessary activities associated with the program. The adequacy of the offeror's project organization to make available the personnel and other resources necessary to carry out the program requirements is evaluated. Also evaluated are the program manager's organizational reporting and communication systems and authority within the company structure, along with the responsibilities of the key positions and the lines of communication and authority. The priority of the proposed effort relative to other company activities is evaluated.
3. Company Resources. The government evaluates the relevance, depth, and diversity of all resources potentially available for contract performance. The government also evaluates the comprehensiveness, responsiveness, and realism of the staffing approach. The evaluation includes the contractor's ability to staff for new requirements from existing resources, recruitment, and temporary assignment when necessary. The critical equipment and facilities proposed for the performance of the contract are also evaluated. The government evaluates the responsibility, education, experience, and availability of the personnel assigned to the major functions associated with the effort.

The relevant experience and past performance evaluation factor includes several subfactors, which can be summarized as follows:

1. Experience. This subfactor considers the nature and magnitude of the offeror's previous and current work and its relation to the work required for the procurement.
2. Technical Performance. This considers the offeror's compliance with technical requirements and performance standards for previous and present work. For hardware systems, this includes compliance with process requirements and control systems as well as the performance requirements for the delivered hardware or system and also whether design life was achieved.
3. Schedule Performance. This subfactor considers how well the contractor has met completion dates. This includes any interim deliverables or milestones such as periodic technical and business reports, system designs, and prototype hardware.
4. Cost Performance. This subfactor considers cost increases and cost savings experienced on previous and current contracts. In assessing cost performance, customer directed efforts to mitigate cost increases are also evaluated.

Other considerations are also taken into account in the evaluation of an offer. They include the financial condition and capability of the offeror, labor-management relations, and business systems.

The section of the solicitation on the Statement of Work (SOW) is a complex one in the context of a procurement for a highly technical item. In the sample solicitation being reviewed here the object of the procurement are transponders and related items for the Goddard Space Flight Center (GSFC).

Under the management, reporting, and documentation heading of the Statement of Work, there are several requirements. The contractor must designate a single individual who will be given full responsibility and authority to manage and administer all phases of the work. The contractor must provide for managing of all resources; controlling schedules; managing all engineering, manufacturing, and procurement activities; configuration management, quality assurance, documentation control, and distribution. The contractor must also prepare and present to the GSFC a weekly project review and a monthly written report. The report must be a summary presentation of the progress, problem areas, and activities on-going and planned, including status of procurements, personnel changes, and the like. The contractor is also required to prepare a quarterly project review between award contract and hardware delivery.

The contractor is required to follow a GSFC-approved Configuration Management Plan and must control the design and hardware, by means of drawings, specifications, and other documents, and must classify all changes as Class I or Class II. Class I changes are defined as those affecting the contract schedule, performance, the agreed-to-baseline configuration, safety, interfaces, or change to approved documents. Class I changes require written GSFC written approval prior to implementation. Class II changes are controlled and dispositioned by the contractor, although the GSFC reserves the right to review all Class II changes for technical content to ensure the proper classification has been assigned.

The contractor is required to plan, conduct, and document internal design reviews for the hardware. Reviews must be conducted by personnel not directly involved in the hardware under review. Summaries of these reviews are to be included in the project status reports. Prior to committing any design to manufacturing, the contractor must conduct a detailed review of the design to ensure that all requirements, such as electrical/electronic, grounding, shielding, harness layout, structural, thermal, venting, contamination, fabrication/assembly, and process requirements, are satisfied.

Under the engineering provisions, the contractor is required to perform analyses of system requirements. The analyses are designed to ensure the compatibility of the transponder with itself and the GSFC spacecraft for each environment to be encountered throughout use including operating and nonoperating conditions during ground operations, the transportation environment, the spacecraft launch environment, and the on-orbit environment. Among the items to be analyzed are the following:

a. electrical and electronic design;
b. thermal engineering;
c. structural engineering; and
d. electrical, electronic, and electromechanical parts engineering.

Other requirements for the contractor are listed in the Hardware Fabrication, Assembly, and Test heading of the Statement of Work. It is the contractor's duty to fabricate, assemble, inspect, and test the transponder. He must generate all necessary procedures to test the hardware and its components or subassemblies. In particular, the contractor must verify and document through appropriate tests, inspections, and analyses that the hardware assemblies have been fabricated and assembled in accordance with the controlling documentation and that the performance is in accordance with applicable specifications. The contractor must also document all anomalies, nonconformances and failures, and their disposition on nonconformance reports. Appropriate controlling documentation for the item, such as drawings and specifications, must reflect the as-designed, as-built, as-inspected, as-tested configurations of hardware before the hardware is moved to its next scheduled station.

The Quality Assurance heading of the SOW requires the contractor to establish an organized program that will demonstrate that the design meets the functional requirements, including specified margins; has been manufactured properly; and will operate properly in association with all specified parameters. The contractor is further required to implement and maintain a performance assurance program that encompasses all flight equipment, including flight spares and government-furnished flight equipment.

NOTES

1. In general, see George V. d'Angelo, *Aerospace Agencies and Organizations, a Guide for Business and Government*, Quorum Books, Westport, Conn., 1993.

2. Stephen Kahn, *Advanced Technology Projects and International Procurement: The Case of the European Space Agency*, 2 Public Procurement Law Review, 1993, at 13.

3. Procurement Guidelines under financial assistance from the International Fund for Agricultural Development, § 1.3.

4. *Id.*, § 1.4.
5. *Id.*, § 2.3.
6. *Id.*, § 2.4.
7. *Id.*, § 2.9.
8. *Id.*, § 2.10.
9. ESA/C (82) 111, approved by the ESA Council of Ministers in 1982, revised in 1988.
10. Kahn, *supra*, at 17.
11. *Ibid.*, at 19.
12. *Id.*, at 24.
13. *Id.*, at 28.
14. *Id.*, at 30.
15. Article 4 – Principles of the Contract Regulations.
16. Kahn, *supra*, at 37.
17. Form GC/Stores/1 Edition of April 1979.
18. 48 CFR 1.101.
19. At § 1.301 *et seq.*
20. 41 U.S.C. 418b § 22.
21. 32 CFR 160.4(a).
22. Part 5301 § 9001.
23. *Id.*, § 9003–2.
24. Navy Acquisition Procedures Supplement, 1992 edition, Part 5201.690–§§ 1 through 9.
25. Materials made available by David P. Forbes, Associate General Counsel, National Aeronautics and Space Administration, 1993.

Chapter Four

Insurance

HISTORY OF SPACECRAFT INSURANCE

Insurance for space activities has developed after many years of work by aerospace clients, brokers, and the worldwide underwriting community. The objective of that work was to provide flexible forms of insurance for a volatile class of exposure, not yet quantified by loss data and experience in the field.[1]

Insurance coverage for a commercial spacecraft was first placed in 1965 for the Early Bird satellite (INTELSAT I) for third-party liability. At the time, it was not possible to purchase coverage for launch and in-orbit risks because the underwriting community knew very little about rocket technology and did not possess sufficient data to set premium rates.[2] After six attempts to place satellites into orbit, two of which failed, INTELSAT III F-1 was lost and underwriters began to compile information on satellites and launch vehicles in order to develop a better understanding of the risks involved in this type of activity. It was 1968 and space commerce was still in its infancy. COMSAT (the Communications Satellite Corporation) wanted to insure its interest in the launches of the remaining INTELSAT III satellites and approached the three leading aviation underwriters, the London Market, Associated Aviation Underwriters (AAU), and United States Aviation Underwriters (USAU). The underwriters analyzed the risks of launching commercial satellites and were, at first, reluctant to accept launch failures as an acceptable risk. After further evaluation of hardware reliability and in-orbit satellite survivability, the London Market and Associated Aviation Underwriters agreed to insure the remaining INTELSAT III launches against launch failure.

Because the insurance market was unwilling to provide launch failure coverage on a first-loss basis, a deductible provision was incorporated allowing one launch failure out of a total of five launches. INTELSAT III F-2, F-3, and F-4 were launched successfully. INTELSAT III F-5 failed due to launch vehicle malfunction and the series was extended to include an additional satellite. The policy was rewritten to accommodate the additional launch. The last satellite in the series, INTELSAT III F-8, failed, but no claim was presented to the underwriters because of the one-failure deductible.

In 1971 a new launch series began with the INTELSAT IV program. As with insurance for the previous series, only COMSAT's interest in the program was covered. There was some new thinking, however, in terms of the type and scope of insurance coverage needed. INTELSAT III F-7 had reached its intended orbital position and the launch qualified as a success, but the satellite's operational life was shortened by a fuel problem. The definition of launch failure, therefore, had to be modified.

INTELSAT IV involved a series of eight satellites for which a policy was sought with a two-launch failure deductible. In addition to London and AAU, this time USAU also agreed to underwrite the INTELSAT IV program. The amount of space insurance market capacity thus doubled to almost $9 million. The first six of the eight launches were successful and the policy automatically terminated in December 1974. The last two launches were then insured with a one-failure deductible out of a two-launch policy.

In 1975 the government of Canada purchased launch and satellite liability coverage for its ANIK satellite series. It was the first time that a government had purchased insurance for its satellites. The European Space Agency (ESA) and the Indian Department of Space (DOS) also purchased insurance for their systems. Later, satellite insurance was purchased by the governments of Indonesia, Brazil, Australia, and others. During the same period, RCA Corporation purchased satellite life insurance for the first of its SATCOM series of satellites. That event was a turning point because it was the first attempt to determine the in-orbit reliability of a commercial satellite. It was clear to both spacecraft operators and underwriters that in-orbit failure could be as devastating as launch failure. A partial failure clause was eventually added to deal with subsystems failure, including excessive loss of station-keeping fuel, loss of electrical power generation or storage systems, or transponder breakdown. Since then, many governments and private firms have purchased prelaunch, launch, and satellite life insurance for their communications satellite systems. Among them are American Telephone and Telegraph (AT&T), the European Space Agency, the European Telecommunications Satellite Organization (EUTELSAT), General Telephone and Electric (GTE), Home Box Office (HBO), TELESAT of Canada; the National Space Agency of Japan (NASDA), and Western Union.

In the ten years or so from the late seventies until the late eighties, spacecraft insurance saw a period of uncertainty and shrinking capacity due to many failures and accidents. In 1977 the European Space Agency lost a valuable test satellite. The next year it was the turn of the Japanese Space Agency to lose a satellite. Another big loss followed in 1979 with RCA's SATCOM III failing to achieve the proper orbit. By 1980, the loss ratio for spacecraft insurance was over 200 percent and every insurance underwriter was reevaluating this business. After a brief recovery of the satellite insurance business in the early eighties, due mostly to the entrance into the business of marine and other insurance underwriters, several launch and in-orbit losses resulted in insurance claim payments of $100 million. In 1984 there were more losses resulting in underwriting payments of over $290 million and a loss ratio of 300 percent. 1986 saw the Challenger accident, which resulted in the destruction of the orbiter and the death of the crew members, the grounding of the entire Shuttle fleet, and the transfer of all future payloads to the commercial launch vehicle industry. In April 1986, a Titan 34D rocket failed and destroyed a valuable government payload, a loss followed the next month by the failure of a Delta payload. Other losses followed involving the Ariane launcher.

Starting in May 1988, after a period of two years, Ariane resumed its launch operations with three launches and the U.S. commercial launch vehicles flew their first commercial satellites. Resumption of successful launches helped reestablish underwriters' confidence in the space business, increased premium flow to the insurance market, and the premium rates dropped from 20 percent to 16.5 to 17 percent. Loss ratios, which had reached a high of 300 percent in 1984, dropped to 150 percent in 1990.

INSURANCE COVERAGE TODAY

After more than 20 years of experience, spacecraft insurance policies have become quite sophisticated. New types of coverage are being developed for private launch vehicle companies, remote-sensing spacecraft, and space materials processing. Each policy, however, is an individual contract resulting from negotiations between spacecraft operators and their insurers and are tailored to the particular situation and needs of the parties. More than 50 spacecraft insurance programs have been used worldwide.

Although it is impossible to make a list of all the issues a contract can address, we can examine a typical launch insurance policy to get a general sense of how spacecraft operators and underwriters handle risk factors. Before we do that, however, it is essential to understand what the general categories of risk are. The basic types of coverage reflect the operational stages of a spacecraft's life. They are preignition coverage, launch coverage, in-orbit coverage, and liability coverage.

The preignition insurance is a coverage designed to indemnify the owner during the manufacture, storage, transit, and integration phase. In many cases, when the satellite is a spare, the storage provision in the contract between the purchaser and the manufacturer will specifically require insurance coverage. Coverage terminates with the intentional ignition of the launch engines. Indeed, intentional ignition is also a crucial threshold because it often marks the transfer of risk between the manufacturer of a spacecraft and the owner or operator.

The launch coverage itself starts at intentional ignition of the launch vehicle and usually lasts for 180 days thereafter. During that phase, coverage includes the cost of a replacement spacecraft, the cost of relaunch services, lost revenue, and cost of insurance. Companies such as General Dynamics, Martin Marietta, McDonnell Douglas and Arianespace offer so-called launch risk guarantees. Launch service providers "guarantee" the performance of their launch vehicle at insurance rates comparable to those offered by conventional insurers. The advantage of guarantees is that they guarantee capacity up to three years or more prior to launch.

The in-orbit coverage begins where launch coverage terminates, that is, usually 180 days after launch. Spacecraft liability insurance covers third-party claims incurred during the launch phase and throughout the operational life of the satellite.

Moving to the actual launch insurance policy,[3] we find a section on the declarations, in which the basic features of the agreement are spelled out. The activities of the insured are described. The policy period and the sum insured are specified as regards each specific satellite. The termination of risk is also defined. Namely, risk of loss, for each satellite where attachment of risk has occurred, is to terminate on the earliest of the following: (a) when the satellite is agreed to be a total loss or a constructive total loss, (b) when agreed claims equal the sum insured, (c) at the time of expiration of the policy, or (d) at launch termination. Launch termination or launch delay is also specified in the contract. The satellite(s) and the launch vehicle are then described and the scheduled launch date is specified.

A standard launch delay provision would read as follows:

In the case of a launch delay for a satellite exceeding three months beyond its scheduled launch date, the Insured is entitled at three months from date of receipt by Insurers of the premium for that satellite to call for reimbursement of the premium for that satellite without interest, and this policy shall remain in force, provided that, and until such time as, a new launch date is established to occur within the policy period.

A launch termination/reinstatement provision could be drafted as follows:

In the event of a launch termination, coverage under this policy shall suspend. In the event of a launch termination such that a subsequent launch of the satellite can occur, the insurers agree to reinstate coverage under this policy, for such subsequent launch, subject to conditions.

In order for coverage to be reinstated following a launch termination, the insured must normally provide a certification it has received from the manufacturer of the satellite and the launch service provider that no damage to the satellite has occurred. In the event damage has occurred to the satellite and/or launch vehicle, the insured must provide to the insurers a detailed description of the damage and of the actions, such as handling, rework, and retest, to which the satellite or launch vehicle were subjected in conjunction with the identification and remedy of the damages and the validation of the repairs. If a satellite is removed from the launch vehicle and then reintegrated therewith, the insured must provide insurers a full explanation and a detailed description of the handling, storage, and revalidation tests to which the satellite and/or launch vehicle has been subjected as part of this process. If a satellite has been removed from the launch vehicle or been damaged, certification must be provided, prior to any subsequent intentional ignition that the damage, if any, has been satisfactorily repaired and, if removal has occurred, that the satellite has been reintegrated on the launch vehicle in compliance with the original contract specifications and that the launch vehicle is flight ready.

The next part of the contract sets forth the insuring agreements. Typically, the insurers agree with the insureds that

a. in the event of a total loss or constructive total loss of the satellite, the insurers will pay the sum insured;
b. in the event of a partial loss, they will indemnify the insured as determined in the contract; or

c. in the event of launch termination not resulting in a total or constructive total loss, they will indemnify the insureds for those extra expenses and/or damages directly resulting from the launch termination.

If there is a loss indemnifiable under the policy that, within reasonable time, can be satisfactorily corrected or compensated for by additional ground installation, procedural changes, software development, or any other means, the insurers have the option to either indemnify the insured or bear all the necessary expenses incurred by the insured as a result of the corrective measures. If the insurers opt for the corrective measures, but those measures fail to achieve satisfactory correction, the insurers will bear all the expenses related to the corrective measures, in addition to the amount of indemnification for the satellite.

The next section of the launch insurance agreement deals with the definitions. Although definitions are important in every contract, they are essential in this particular context because of the technology involved and the enormous consequences deriving from the passage of risk from one party to another.

Available transponder years means the cumulative sum of the available transponder life remaining for all transponders. Transponder life is the number of years during which each transponder will be available to operate in accordance with the satellite performance specifications. If because of power, fuel, or other deficiencies, it can be determined that a transponder, even though functioning correctly at the time of initial operation, will later experience transponder failure, then the point of predicted cessation of operation is considered to be the end of available transponder life for that transponder.

Intentional ignition, an event of crucial importance, is defined as "the act of intentionally igniting the first stage engines of the launch vehicle for the purpose of launch." Launch is normally defined as "the intentional ignition and subsequent release of the table clamps which secure the launch vehicle to the launch pad." Launch termination means that point in time when, following intentional ignition, the first stage main engines of the launch vehicle shut down before launch and the launch pad is officially declared safe.

Satellite performance specifications are contained in the policy. A transponder is defined to mean "that combination of connected elements within the overall communications subsystem of the satellite that taken together provide a transmission capability."

Transponder failure is intended as the physical loss of, or damage to, or failure of the transponder or of the satellite of which it is a part, to meet the satellite performance specifications, such that the insured, using reasonable business judgment and after examining all technical alternatives for correcting the failure, determines that the transponder cannot be used for the intended commercial communications of the insured. The insured is required to use all available redundant components before any transponder is considered a transponder failure.

Total loss, or constructive total loss, is defined as the occurrence of transponder failures such that the available transponder years are 50 percent or less of the stated transponder years. Partial loss means the occurrence of a transponder failure that does not result in a total or constructive total loss. The indemnity afforded under the typical policy for a partial loss is determined by multiplying the sum insured by the partial loss factor (PLF). The PLF is calculated by dividing the available transponder years by the stated transponder years. Available and stated transponder years are determined at the same point in time. In the event the insured claims a partial loss for which the preceding PLF does not apply, the indemnity will reflect the actual loss suffered by the insured and, when possible, will be determined by mutual agreement of both parties.

The conditions section of the launch insurance policy is usually rather standard. It includes provisions on the notice and proof of loss, payment of claims, due diligence, fraud or misrepresentation, subrogation, and cancellation. An arbitration clause is normally included. It can either be with the International Chamber of Commerce or the American Arbitration Association. The policy also selects the applicable law.

The exclusions section of the policy contains some standard provisions such as acts of God, war, insurrection, strikes, and civil commotion. It also excludes coverage for confiscation by order of any government or agency or public authority whether secret or otherwise. Also excluded from coverage are losses resulting from anti-satellite devices, or device employing atomic or nuclear fission and/or fusion, or device employing laser or directed energy beams. Losses are also not covered if they are the result of nuclear reaction, nuclear radiation, or radioactive contamination of any nature, except for radiation naturally occurring in the space environment. Loss of revenue, extra expenses, and incidental and consequential damages are not usually covered under this type of insurance policy. Also, third-party liability is not covered and spacecraft operators purchase a policy specifically designed to cover that type of liability.

LIABILITY INSURANCE

With the development of commercial space transportation, issues of risk management are very important in view of the considerable financial commitments of launch participants and the enormity of losses that may occur.[4] In addition to the risk involved in the loss or failure of spacecraft that we have seen, space transportation creates exposure to potentially astronomical liability to third parties injured by the malfunctioning spacecraft or rocket boosters. As an example of the type of risk posed by space activities, consider the 1989 launch of the Galileo interplanetary explorer. The Galileo is a nuclear fueled satellite that was carried into outer space aboard the space Shuttle Atlantis. Although the in-orbit stage of Galileo is a short one, it still presents many dangers. A launch accident or unplanned re-entry of that type of craft could result in significant radioactive contamination of the earth's atmosphere or surface. If the space shuttle Challenger, which exploded only 74 seconds after liftoff, carried a nuclear power source and the fuel protective capsule would have ruptured in the explosion, it might have caused dispersion of radioactive debris on a large tract of the east coast of Florida.[5]

Private industry risked no liability for the Galileo launch because it was a government project. Nevertheless, the Challenger accident demonstrates that private firms will increasingly face that type of risk. Because progress in space transportation involves compact, powerful, and reliable power sources, the use of nuclear power sources may some day become essential and liability exposure will acquire enormous dimensions. In fact, even without the use of nuclear energy, a privately owned large-sized spacecraft can present a potential hazard to third parties all over the world.[6]

Companies involved in aerospace activities face potential tort liability both domestically and internationally. The applicable domestic law of the United States currently consists of federal regulations and common law tort theory, as well as relevant state laws. Liability under international law is established primarily through several treaties. Companies may also be subject to the various tort laws of foreign countries in which their spacecraft happens to cause damage or whose citizens are harmed by the operation of the craft. The applicable U.S. tort theories include strict liability for an abnormally dangerous activity, negligence and *res ipsa loquitur.*[7] A company involved in space activities must therefore analyze domestic law, international treaties, and some foreign statutes as well.

The policy of the U.S. government is and has been for some time to encourage the development of space commerce and, particularly, space transportation. The government realized, however, that the risk of liability accompanying space activities could inhibit the space launch industry's progress. Maintaining a liability structure that would not subject entrepreneurs to excessive damages was therefore considered essential to encourage further development.

With a view to promote economic growth and entrepreneurial activity in launch vehicle transportation, in 1984 Congress passed the *Commercial Space Launch Act.*[8] The Department of Transportation was officially assigned to oversee and coordinate the conduct of commercial launch operations and the Office of Commercial Space Transportation (OCST) was established within the DOT to carry out the space responsibilities of the department.

Under the terms of the act, as was passed in 1984, the OCST had authority to "establish requirements for liability insurance, hold harmless agreements, proof of financial responsibility, and such other assurances as may be needed to protect the United States and its agencies and personnel from liability, loss or injury as a result of a launch or operation of a launch site involving Government facilities or personnel."[9] The act also required that any person involved in launch activities under a license issued pursuant to the act have in effect liability insurance in an amount determined by the OCST to be necessary for such operations "considering the international obligations of the United States."[10] The OCST was required to set appropriate levels of risk assumption, but at the same time it did not want to discourage the private sector from providing commercial launch services. Companies that had the capability of providing launch services had until then operated as government contractors and enjoyed government indemnification for any liability arising from launch accidents. In this new private launch business, U.S. companies had to assume unlimited liability risks and also found themselves at a disadvantage compared to foreign government owned or controlled launch service providers.[11]

The commercial launch industry, concerned by unlimited liability and foreign competition, solicited government intervention. After a long process of discussions by congressional committees, hearings, industry interventions, and draft bills, the *Commercial Space Launch Act Amendments of 1988* were passed.[12] The intent of those amendments was to stimulate the growth of world insurance markets so that they would meet the needs of the domestic launch industry. In the words of the Senate Committee on Commerce, Science and Transportation:

> The Government . . . must act as a reliable partner and be willing to provide transitional support to this nascent industry until such time as equitable "rules of the road" are in place and the insurance industry has the capability to accommodate the increased insurance requirements of commercial space activities at reasonable rates.[13]

The amendments include several provisions concerning a licensee's liability to third parties. The definition of "third party" is limited as follows:

"third party" means a person or entity other than—

a. the United States, its agencies, or its contractors or subcontractors involved in launch services;
b. the licensee or transferee;
c. the licensee's or transferee's contractors, subcontractors, or customers involved in launch services; or
d. any such customer's contractors or subcontractors involved in launch services.[14]

The definition excludes government employees and contractors as third parties. It also excludes private employees and contractors who are involved directly with the actual launch. The importance of this exclusion is apparent if one considers that serious injury and property damage are most likely to occur on or near the launch facility at or soon after lift-off. The amendment's provisions limiting liability for third-party injuries do not apply to this high-risk group.[15]

The secretary of transportation was obligated by the amendments to Section 15(c) to require assurances to protect the United States, its agencies, and personnel from liability, death, bodily injury, or loss of or damage to property resulting from a launch or operation of a launch site involving government facilities or personnel. The Department of Transportation now has paramount authority to determine the responsibility to be assumed by launch companies. It is, however, foreclosed from relieving the government of liability for loss or injury arising as a result of willful misconduct of the United States or its agents.[16]

Section 16 of the original act only required a launch company to have liability insurance in such amount as the secretary deemed necessary in view of the treaty obligations of the United States. The amended version is much more extensive. It requires launch companies to have insurance or to demonstrate financial responsibility of two types. The launch company must first obtain insurance or demonstrate financial responsibility "in an amount sufficient to compensate the maximum probable loss . . . from claims by a third party for death, bodily injury, or loss of or damage to property resulting from activities carried out under the license."[17] The "maximum probable loss" is determined by the secretary after consultation with the heads of NASA, the Air Force, and other agencies as appropriate. Such an insurance or responsibility is not to exceed $500 million or "the maximum liability insurance available on the world market at a reasonable cost."[18] The second type of insurance or financial responsibility which a launch company must demonstrate must be "in an amount sufficient to compensate the maximum probable loss from claims against any person by the United States for loss or damage to property of the United States resulting from activities under the license."[19] The maximum insurance or responsibility required is not to exceed $100 million or whatever amount is available on world insurance markets at reasonable cost.

The mentioned maximum amounts of insurance are to be reviewed by the Department of Transportation within 6 months of the amendment of the act and every 12 months thereafter.[20] The secretary may propose adjustments to adapt to "altered liability expectations and availability of insurance on the world market."[21] The secretary must submit the proposed adjustments to Congress but he retains full discretion in determining insurance levels because his decision cannot be overridden. He even has discretion to permit a launch in the complete absence of insurance.[22] He is also authorized to pay for third-party claims exceeding any insurance or financial responsibility a launch company has in place, up to $1.5 billion, resulting from activities carried out under a license.[23]

According to the Senate Report accompanying the amendments, the provision regarding insurance requirements for "claims against any person by the United States for loss of or damage to property of the United States" refers to property insurance to protect the United States from loss of government property.[24] It is not clear, however, as to whether "property of the United States" includes just property owned by the United States or all property used by the government in connection with the operation of the launch site. The safest approach for a launch company would probably be to purchase a type of all risk property insurance for and on behalf of the government with the government named as the insured. An alternative to that approach could be to extend existing liability insurance to include coverage for damage caused to government property.[25]

The most important section of the amendments provides that the United States will pay successful claims of a third party against the licensee resulting from the licensee's space launch activities, "for death, bodily injury, or loss of or damage to property" if "the aggregate of . . . claims arising out of any particular launch: (A) is in excess of the amount of insurance or demonstration of financial responsibilities required . . . and . . . (B) is not in excess of the level that is $1,500,000,000 . . . above such amount."[26] The effect of that provision is that the U.S. government will pay any successful damage claims by third parties in excess of $500 million but less than $2 billion. Any amount over that will be the responsibility of the licensee. An exception to the government's duty to pay compensation above the $500 million level is willful misconduct of the licensee.[27]

The amendments also specify some conditions for payment by the United States. Notice to the government of any claim arising from a particular launch is required, as is the government's opportunity to participate in the defense of a licensee, and approval from the secretary of transportation for release of appropriate funds.[28] It is important to understand, however, that indemnification is not assured. It is only provided if appropriations acts have been enacted in advance to provide authority for the payments of claims.

RECIPROCAL WAIVERS OF CLAIMS

The liability insurance section of the 1988 amendments requires the establishment of reciprocal waivers of claims among all the entities participating in launch activities. The Senate Report accompanying the amendments notes that the purpose of this requirement is "(1) to limit the total universe of claims that might arise as a result of a launch; and (2) to eliminate the necessity for all of these parties to obtain property and casualty insurance to protect against these claims."[29] The waivers are to be entered into by participants "involved in launch services" and must extend to damage or loss "resulting from activities carried out under the license."

The effect of the reciprocal waiver requirement is that each launch company, its contractors and subcontractors, the launch customer, its contractors and subcontractors, and the government with its own contractors and subcontractors, agree to assume any risk of loss, damage, bodily injury, or death. An express condition of the launch license is that waivers flow to each of the licensee's contractors, subcontractors, and customers.[30] Essentially, the licensee and any other organization assisting in the actual launch will be immune from the others' claims. Therefore, by agreement, the licensee's insurance will cover losses incurred by any of these organizations during the launch operation, regardless of fault.[31]

This type of waiver scheme has been largely used in commercial space activities since the first NASA launches, and has been adopted by every major launch service provider operating today. To ensure that the scheme serves its purpose, however, care must be taken by the government and the licensee to ensure that their respective contractors accept the waiver and pass it along to their own subcontractors.[32] Although the government is under the same waiver obligation, the secretary is not permitted to waive any claims on behalf of government employees and their rights are not affected.[33] Government employees would in fact be considered third parties under the amendments definition and would benefit under the third-party liability insurance requirement.[34] Also, any waiver required of the government only applies to the amount in excess of the $100 million financial responsibility limit for government property insurance.

As part of its financial responsibility licensing order the OCST has incorporated an "Agreement for Waiver of Claims and Assumption of Responsibility." The agreement is a three-party contract among the licensee, its customer, and the government, where both the licensee and the customer waive and release claims either may have against the other, the government, and the contractors and subcontractors of the foregoing, for losses resulting from licensed launch activities. At the same time, the government agrees to waive and release claims it may have in excess of the insurance or financial responsibility required by the act.[35]

EUROPE

The Space Centre at Kourou in French Guyana is managed by three entities:

1. the European Space Agency, which owns the majority of the equipment at the launch site, and has responsibility for the general management of the Ariane program and the financing for construction works;
2. the Centre National d'Études Spatiales (CNES), the French Space Agency which is responsible for the construction and coordination of operations of the centre; and
3. Arianespace, a company in charge of the marketing of launch services, the management and the financing for the construction of launch vehicles.

In the event of loss or damage resulting from a launch accident, liability rests with the preceding entities. The exact allocation of responsibility is not specifically regulated.[36] For what concerns the risk of loss of or damage to the property of CNES, ESA, or Arianespace, or loss of life or injury to their employees, Arianespace provides specific guarantees. An understanding is in force to the effect that, after using the launch facilities, Arianespace must return them in the same condition in which it found them. Arianespace is also required to purchase insurance coverage for an amount equal to or greater than the value of the facilities. An agreement is in force between CNES and ESA that includes a reciprocal waiver for claims without the right of subrogation, an arrangement similar to those described for the United States.

NOTES

1. Edward Ridley, Jr., and Amanda Lee Moore, *Astrobusiness, a Guide to the Commerce and Law of Outer Space*, Praeger Publishers, New York, 1985, p. 37.

2. The insurance history section of this chapter is, in part, a summary of *A Report on Spacecraft Insurance*, by Johnson and Higgins, New York Insurance Brokers.

3. Draft policy of satellite launch insurance, kindly provided by International Space Brokers, Inc., of Virginia, 1993.

4. Peter D. Nesgos, *Commercial Space Transportation: A New Industry Emerges*, XVI Annals of Air and Space Law, 1991, p. 402.

5. Van C. Ern, *Third Party Liability of the Private Space Industry: To Pay What No One Has Paid Before*, 41 Case Western Reserve Law Review 1991, pp. 504–505.

6. *Id.*

7. Bosco, *Manufacturer Liability to Third Parties for Outer Space Activities*, 7 Northrop U.L.J. 1, 1986, pp. 30–51, in Ern, *supra* at 506.

8. Pub. L. 98–575; 49 U.S.C. 2601, enacted on October 30, 1984.

9. Id., Sec. 15 (3).

10. *Id.*, Sec. 16. See also Peter D. Nesgos, *Recent Developments in Risk Allocation of Concern to the U.S. Commercial Launch Industry and the Insurance Community*, remarks at the Assicurazioni Generali Fifth International Conference on Space Insurance, Rome, March 2–3, 1989.

11. See Nesgos, *supra*, at p. 4.

12. Pub. L. 100–657, October, 1988, signed into law on November 15, 1988.

13. Report of the Senate Committee on Commerce, Science and Transportation on H.R. 4399, 100th Cong., 2nd Sess., Report 100–593, Government Printing Office, Washington, D.C., 1988, at p. 3.

14. 49 U.S.C. § 2603(11) (1988).

15. Ern, *supra*, at 511.

16. Section 15(c) of the Commercial Launch Act as amended. Also see Nesgos, *supra*, at 405.

17. Sec. 16(a)(1)(A) of the amended act.

18. *Ibid.*

19. Sec. 16(a)(1)(B) of the act as amended.

20. Sec. 16(A)(4).

21. *Ibid.*

22. Senate Report, *supra*, note 36, at 9, 10, in Nesgos, *supra*, at 406.

23. Sec. 16(a)(1)(B) of the amended act.

24. Senate Report, *supra*, note 36 at 12.

25. Nesgos, *supra*, at 408.

26. 49 U.S.C. § 2615(b)(1), in Ern, *supra*, at 513.

27. *Id.*

28. *Id.*, § 2615(b)(2).

29. Senate Report, *supra*, p. 14.

30. Nesgos, *supra*, at 408.
31. Ern, *supra*, at 512.
32. Nesgos, *supra*, at 408.
33. Senate Report, *supra*, note 36 at 14.
34. Sec. 4(11) of the amended act, and Sec. 16(a)(1)(B).
35. Nesgos, *supra*, at 410.
36. Stephane Lessard and Frederic Nordlund, *Le Base de Lancement: Évolution et Aspects Juridiques*, XV Annals of Air and Space Law, XV 1990, p. 387.

Chapter Five

Satellite Communications

Life as we know it today would be impossible without satellite communication. More than at any time in history, today satellites provide us with instant visual access to events anywhere in the world. To a large extent, satellites also handle basic services such as telephone traffic, telex, and other vital communications. An explosive growth of the information industries has created enormous demand for transmission services that must accommodate the increasingly large use of computer modems, cellular phones, and other related equipment.[1]

The increasing demand for communication service results in the corresponding scarcity of available electromagnetic spectrum, which must then be efficiently allocated and managed. Planning and allocation of the frequency spectrum at the international level are coordinated by mechanisms of the International Telecommunications Union (ITU), a specialized agency of the United Nations. In Europe, that function is assumed by the European Conference of Postal and Telecommunications Administration (CEPT). Also, as part of its new telecommunications initiative, the Commission of the European Economic Community is assuming a new role as a coordinating and policy-formulating body on frequency allocation in Europe. In the United States, spectrum is managed by the Federal Communications Commission. In accordance with its mandate, issuing from the *Communications Act* of 1934,[2] the FCC is in charge of determining which competing users receive certain valuable spectrum. In doing so, it must consider the public interest, convenience, and necessity.

At the national level, assignments of frequencies to specific users are based on national tables of frequency allocations. The national tables are drawn up on the basis of the international table of frequency allocations.

National tables may only deviate from the international one according to the conditions and specifications of the ITU's Radio Regulations. In most countries, the process of drawing national tables of frequency allocations is organized in the form of a consultative procedure, where interested parties can formulate their interest to the regulatory authority.[3]

THE UNITED STATES

Filing Domestic Satellite Earth Station Applications

Public Notices issued by the FCC are designed to provide applicants with information that will increase the likelihood of filing successful earth station applications. Public Notice Report No. DS-1231[4] outlines the guidelines for filing domestic satellite earth station applications. In addition to the instructions on how to fill out the prescribed forms, the notice addresses the problem of safety and radiation exposure associated with the operation of earth stations and issues guidelines for the FCC Satellite Radio Branch.

When applying for a license to construct and operate an earth station, licensees must certify whether grant of the application may have a significant environmental impact as defined by the *Commission's Rules*.[5] In making this determination, the applicant must determine whether the proposed facility is categorically deemed to have a potential significant effect or whether the guidelines for radio frequency radiation levels are exceeded. If either of these determinations are affirmative, the applicant must submit an environmental assessment with its application. In order for an applicant to make a proper certification with regard to radiofrequency radiation levels, the applicant should prepare a radiation hazard study in advance of filing the application. The radiation evaluation should consider the contributions to power density levels of any nearby noncategorically excluded transmitters that could add significantly to potential exposure levels. If there are no potential hazards and no applicable limits are exceeded, the applicant may certify no significant environmental effect on the appropriate form. If, however, there is a potential hazard, applicants must submit an environmental assessment containing a summary table and a statement to the effect that no risks exist for the region under consideration. If, in spite of the applicant's statement, the facility is found to exceed the applicable radio frequency radiation guidelines, the commission may request the licensee to submit its radiation hazard study. If misrepresentation is found, the applicant may be subject to forfeiture.

Operational and technical requirements for earth stations have changed during the last several years. For example, earth stations licensed after January

1, 1986, must meet a more stringent electromagnetic radiation standard than those stations licensed before that date. Renewal and modification applications afford the FCC the opportunity to assess whether older stations are in compliance with the new requirements. All applications for modification and renewal of earth stations must now include the correct emission designator for the station in accordance with the commission's rules. Other requirements are stressed with regard to standards for multiple antenna facilities.

Filing Applications for Space Station Authorization

An applicant for a space station authorization must submit a comprehensive proposal for each proposed space station in narrative form and attach exhibits with the information described below. A separate application should be filed for each space station to be constructed.

Each application for a new or modified space station authorization must constitute a concrete proposal for commission evaluation, although the applicant may propose alternatives that increase flexibility in accommodating the satellite in orbit. Each application must also contain the formal waiver required by Section 304 of the *Communications Act*.[6] The technical information for a proposed satellite radio system need not be filed on any specific form but should be complete in all pertinent details. Among the information required to be furnished in each application are the following:

1. type of authorization requested (e.g., construction permit, launch authority, station license, or modification of authorization);
2. general description of the overall system facilities, operations, and services;
3. radio frequencies and polarization plan, center frequency and polarization of transponders, emission designators and allocated bandwidth of emission, final amplifier output power, identification of which antenna beams are connected or switchable to each transponder, receiving system noise temperature, and other channel details;
4. orbital location requested for the satellite, the factors that support such an orbital assignment, the range of orbital locations from which adequate service can be provided, and a detailed explanation of all factors that would limit the orbital arc over which the satellite could adequately serve its expected users;
5. estimated number and geographic distribution of earth stations, and description of proposed arrangements for access to the system between the premises of the users and the earth stations for domestic satellites only;
6. a description of the types of services to be provided, the estimated demand for those services, and the areas and entities to be served, including a description

of the transmission characteristics and performance objectives for each type of proposed service. An estimate of transponder capacity under each of the proposed operating conditions must also be supplied;

7. launch vehicles and arrangements for procuring launch services;
8. physical characteristics of the space station including weight and dimensions of spacecraft, detailed mass (on ground and in orbit) and power budgets, and estimated operational lifetime and reliability of the space station as well as the basis for that estimate:
9. if the request is for additional or replacement satellites, detailed information on the historical use of the system, together with a projection of the types and amount of services for each additional satellite on a year-by-year and transponder-by-transponder basis over the estimated lifetime of the satellite(s);
10. a detailed schedule of the estimated investment costs and operating costs for the proposed system by year, including annual depreciation, maintenance and operating costs, and the basis on which such costs are calculated. Estimated annual revenue requirements should be provided in detail on a year-by-year basis over the estimated design lifetime of the satellites;
11. detailed information demonstrating the financial qualifications of the applicant to construct and launch the proposed satellites;
12. legal qualifications of the applicant;
13. a clear and detailed statement of whether the space station is to be operated on a common carrier basis. If noncommon carrier transactions are proposed, describe the nature of the transactions and specify the number of transponders to be offered on a noncommon carrier basis;
14. dates by which construction will be commenced and completed, launch date, and estimated date of placement into service;
15. applications for international fixed-satellite authorizations shall also provide all information necessary to comply with the policies and procedures set forth in *Establishing of Satellite Systems Providing International Communications*.[7]

Additional information is required for the filing of applications for authorizations in the Radiodetermination Satellite Service. As we see later, more specific and complex requirements govern applications for authorization for mobile satellite service.

Filing Applications for Satellite Systems

As was noted earlier, the general authority of the FCC for telecommunications also includes rule making and licensing for satellite systems. The procedures involved, however, are quite complex in that they involve an intricate web of evolving national policies, requirements of international treaties and obligations, and a multitude of conflicting private interests. Most interactions between satellite companies and the commission fall into one of three categories. The basic one occurs when an applicant seeks a license for a system where spectrum has already been allocated and rules already exist for the licensing of the system. The second category concerns applicants seeking the establishment of a new system. In that case, there are questions of spectrum allocation and service rules. There is also a hybrid category where either service rules or a spectrum allocation need to be created.[8]

The simplest type of application normally requires that a licensing proceeding be conducted to determine the applicant's qualifications or the relative qualifications among competing applicants. Usually, the allocation and service rules for domestic satellites are already in place. Competitors for the same authorization, however, may try to discredit other applicants or existing licensees. The commission then looks at whether the proposal complies with its applicable rules and policies and whether approval of the proposal is generally in the public interest. Entities that want to offer a new service may have to petition for an allocation of spectrum and the creation of rules; they may also have to seek what is known as "pioneer's preference," a classification that gives an advantage in the licensing process to would-be providers of innovative services.[9]

The first step in a new service type of application is the allocation of spectrum. A good illustration, as discussed later, is the ongoing proceedings concerning low-earth orbiting (LEO) satellites. Global spectrum was allocated at the World Administrative Radio Conference (WARC-92) in Spain leaving it to the FCC to distribute the spectrum domestically. A second step in the proceeding is the establishment of licensing rules. After proposed rules are issued, comments are filed by interested parties. After rules are announced, the commission must determine which applicants will be awarded a license. To save time the Commission will often allow applications to be filed before service rules are adopted or spectrum is allocated and will then run both proceedings simultaneously.

As was stated earlier, the FCC can now award pioneer's preference to an applicant who demonstrates technical innovation or proposed unavailable service. A company that receives this type of preference is almost certainly guaranteed a license. When the preference is denied, the usual competition rules apply.

A new procedure now being tested by the FCC is a negotiated rule making where applicants work together to finalize the proposed rules. The idea is to write rules that would permit all of the applicants to operate a system, thereby minimizing conflicts among the applicants during the rule-making and licensing stages of the process.

The process becomes more involved when another entity, such as the ITU, can influence the decision that the agency will make. In these cases, the difficult decision of whether to license other satellite companies to provide public telephone service, or which frequencies to select for low earth satellites, may already have been determined before the FCC becomes involved. In the case of the LEO allocations, for example, the FCC was an active participant at WARC-92, where the initial allocation was made.

The criteria followed by the commission in selecting the most qualified applicant for a satellite license are derived from the *Communications Act*, the *Commission Rules*, and the *Commission Decisions* that interpret the rules. It is important for an applicant to follow those regulations very carefully in order to maximize his chances of being awarded a license. The basic rules are quite obvious. An applicant must be legally, technically, and financially qualified. For example, an applicant must provide details of the costs of constructing and launching its satellite as well as the operating expenses of the first year after launch, and the sources of funds.

The application must be timely filed along with all the supporting documents, such as charts, graphs, and signatures. Most of those materials, however, need only be assembled "substantially." Many defects can actually be corrected after the filing deadline and, when applications are filed in the absence of service rules, the commission will normally allow applicants an opportunity to conform their applications to the final rules, once adopted. The commission, however, is quite strict about missing filing fees, fee forms, and application submission after a cutoff deadline.[10]

In addition to the formalities of the application, the FCC also examines the substance of the proposals. One of the most important assets is the ability of an applicant to share spectrum with others and create a healthy and competitive environment. The so-called "competitive multiple entry" criterion dates back to the "Open Skies" policy of the early 1970s, which sought to attract as many competitors as possible to best serve the public interest.[11]

Once the formalities regarding the filing of the application have been complied with, an applicant can seek an experimental license to prove the reliability of the system it is proposing. If, pursuant to an experimental license, the applicant promotes his system, competing applicants will strive to criticize and find faults in it. Existing licensees may also have an interest in disparaging the proposed new system.

In theory, the commission is bound in its decisions to written rules and regulations and it cannot be influenced by lobbyists or entities of any kind. In reality, however, it seems that it is important to have a good working relationship with the FCC, including the Common Carrier Bureau and the Office of Engineering and Technology, particularly when a new regulatory regime is being proposed for a new service or technology.[12] Because the course of an application for a satellite system is long and complex, from a practical viewpoint the staff of the FCC assumes enormous importance.

The processing of an application begins when it is submitted by the applicant, with fee form and fee, to the Mellon Bank in Pittsburgh. The bank classifies the application by fee code and forwards it to the FCC where copies are sent to the Common Carrier Bureau and to the Office of Engineering and Technology (OET). If the application is for domestic service, it is processed in the Satellite Radio Branch of the Common Carrier Bureau's Domestic Facilities Division. Applications for an international license are sent to the Office of Assistant Bureau Chief, International. When the proposed service is both domestic and international, the processing would normally begin in the domestic branch and then move to the international division. The application in this case would be processed twice.[13]

If there are no problems relating to the formalities related to the fees, the commission will look at the substance of the proposal and focus on the following criteria:

— whether the satellite service would cause interference to other users of the spectrum;

— whether it would create an air hazard; and

— whether it would impose a radiation threat or violate environmental laws.

If the application meets the Commission's legal and technical parameters, the chief of the Common Carrier Bureau will sign it and send it to the full commission for action. In routine situations, such as modifications to an existing license, the chief of the bureau has the authority to grant a license.

The Office of Engineering and Technology evaluates both experimental licenses and pioneer's preference requests. The chief engineer recommends to the full commission whether to grant the requests. Although most experimental proposals are granted, it is not clear whether the grant includes authority to launch a satellite.

There are ways to get around the licensing system, but they are not to be recommended. A typical scheme is the following. If a satellite system is denied, the applicant has the option of applying in another country. If authority to launch a satellite system is granted, it is possible to receive authorization to provide service everywhere, that is, every country except the United States. Because the United States is still the world's largest single market, the drawback is obvious. Of course, an applicant rejected in the United States but licensed abroad may still reapply with the FCC but the prospects for obtaining a license would not be very good in light of the attempt to circumvent the system.[14] Another possibility is the formation of a consortium of applicants where the Commission has determined that the amount of spectrum or the market will support only one licensee. In the past, the commission has approved the formation of a consortium out of several qualified applicants as an innovative decision. This type of arrangement, however, is likely to be legally challenged. In an actual case described in more detail later, the commission authorized the formation of the American Mobile Satellite Corporation (AMSC) in the mobile satellite service field. The FCC had realized that only one license could be granted because of the limited amount of spectrum available. Instead of granting a license to one of the twelve qualified applicants, the commission chose to license the consortium based on the theory that a diverse group would make the best licensee. The commission's ruling was appealed and the Court of Appeals for the District of Columbia Circuit decided that the FCC has authority to create a consortium structure but only if a "compelling justification" could be shown.[15]

Pursuant to a 1984 presidential determination that established separate satellite systems, and to subsequent FCC rulings, these systems have been limited to the long-term lease and sale of space segment capacity for services not interconnected with the public switched telephone network (PSTN). Further, interconnection was permissible only to restore switched services on an emergency basis and if consistent with a 100 circuit exclusion established in 1990 by the government and the commission. The government has now modified its directives and the FCC has recently released new rules that attempt "to broaden the permissible scope of services to be provided over U.S. separate international satellite systems." Under these new rules, separate systems will be allowed to interconnect international private line circuits with the PSTN. The date for the complete elimination of the PSTN restrictions has been set for January 1, 1997. In addition, the new rules will permit separate systems to provide private line service interconnected with the PSTN through the sale or lease of transponder or space segment capacity, video and audio transmission services, emergency restoration services, and up to 100 64–kbps-equivalent circuits for the provision of international telephone service.[16]

Mobile Satellite Services

Mobile satellite services (MSS) are divided domestically and internationally among the aeronautical mobile satellite services (AMSS), the maritime mobile satellite service (MMSS), and the land mobile satellite service (LMSS). The greatest potential for growth is for the land mobile services, which include two-way radio, citizens band radio, cellular telephone, and radio determination service.

Radio determination service is an application of location technology. Land-based services are quite common but are limited by the scope of the terrestrial-based radio waves. Satellites circumvent this problem by increasing the range of the object determination. Radio determination satellite service (RDSS) employs a small transceiver unit that transmits digital pulses to a satellite in geosynchronous orbit. The satellite then retransmits the signal, to the service provider on an electronic map. From that signal the service provider can communicate the location of the truck, ship, or airplane to the user.[17] The majority of land mobile services do not involve satellite communications but the additional scope of satellite services is gradually being recognized and commercially exploited.

Civilian land mobile services began in the United States when NASA, in 1982, petitioned the FCC to set aside a bandwidth for land mobile service experimentation. In 1983 the United States reached an agreement with Canada on the use and coordination of the LMSS in the high ultra-high-frequency (UHF) band. In 1985 the FCC issued a Notice of Proposed Rule Making to establish domestic licensing procedures, encourage development of MSS, and formulate regulatory policies for those services.[18] The notice also invited parties to apply for licenses to construct, launch, and operate MSS systems.[19] The FCC received 12 applications and comments. In July 1986 the commission allocated 27 MHz of spectrum in the L-band for MSS, to be shared with aeronautical mobile satellite services. After receiving 12 MSS applications and related comments the FCC reached six basic conclusions stated in its Second Report and Order.[20] First, the commission decided that there would only be one MSS system, providing aeronautical, maritime, and land mobile satellite services, licensed for the first generation to use the entire allocated bandwidth, both on a primary and secondary basis. Second, in view of the astronomical costs involved in launching a new system, the commission decided to grant a license to a consortium of qualified applicants. Third, each applicant would be required to make a $5 million contribution to the consortium. Fourth, the MSS space segment licensee would be regulated as a nondominant common carrier subject to streamlined tariff filings and facilities authorization procedures. Fifth, the ground segment of the mobile satellite system would be operated by multiple independent licensees that the commission would abstain from regulating. As a final point, the FCC would preempt state regulation of technical standards, entry, and rate regulation of the space segment.

The reason for licensing a consortium was that launching a new communications satellite system was such an expensive and risky operation and the market for MSS so uncertain that it would make sense to spread the risk. The rationale for preempting state regulation was that, although states have some jurisdiction over elements of telecommunication regulation, such as local telephone service rates, the technology was substantially national. Further, the FCC deemed an additional layer of state regulation as potentially stifling. The commission's decision to deregulate the ground segment industry was motivated by the wish to let MSS grow freely. The satellite service was perceived as a vulnerable industry because of its novelty and competition by a strong and well-established terrestrial land mobile service. In order to promote the development of the satellite services, therefore, the FCC promulgated a noninterference policy regarding the ground segment component of the satellite system, which would only be regulated by marketplace forces, subject only to FCC technical specifications. The FCC also supported LMSS growth by placing them in the nondominant common carrier classification, which permitted substantial expediting in its service implementation. The allocation of the generic L-band was designed to promote sharing of the designated band rather than require a rigid allocation of frequencies in independent chunks. The flexibility was intended to avoid the situation where spectrum allocated for one service would prove inadequate whereas the spectrum for another may be underutilized.[21]

Of the 12 qualified MSS applicants, 8 deposited the required $5 million into an escrow account and formed the consortium American Mobile Satellite Company.[22] AMSC is engaging in or proposing several types of service, including (a) voice communications interconnecting land vehicles, boats, and aircraft with the public switched telephone network; (b) mobile radio service, a two-way voice dispatch between a user terminal and a base station; (c) a variety of mobile data services, consisting of two-way data communications that may be combined with the mobile telephone service or with its mobile radio service; (d) a comprehensive aeronautical service consisting of voice and data communications for safety, air traffic control, flight management communications between aircraft and ground facilities, airline administrative communications, and airline passenger communications; (e) telephone and two-way data communications for users in sparsely populated areas using portable terminals at fixed locations; and (f) a satellite-delivered paging service, which would be more powerful and reliable than the land-based paging systems mostly in use today.[23]

As was stated earlier, the ITU is responsible for the development and regulation of international communication. The *ITU Convention* is amended and updated by the Plenipotentiary Conference, which normally meets every five years. When necessary, the ITU convenes Administrative Radio Conferences to deal with special topics that cannot be treated effectively at full plenipotentiary meetings, or at the annual meeting of the Union's Administrative Council. The Administrative Radio Conferences may be for a particular region (RARC) or for the entire world (WARC).

The need to revise the radio regulations to accommodate the requirements of the mobile satellite services was not addressed until 1983 when a specialized conference, WARC-MOB 83 was held in Geneva to deal primarily with distress and safety matters. WARC-MOB 87, held four years later, covered a much broader range of telecommunications matters. The general purpose of this last conference was to review and revise the radio regulations concerning the mobile services, including the mobile satellite services, radio navigation, and radio determination satellite services.

The United States was represented at WARC MOB-87 by the State Department, which coordinates policy recommendations from the FCC and the National Telecommunications Information Administration (NTIA). The Federal Advisory Committee of the FCC recommends policy regarding private sector communications, taking into account international spectrum conflicts, industry growth, and public interest. The NTIA administers the governmental use of spectrum. Through the International Radio Advisory Committee, the NTIA ensures that all government users, including defense, have sufficient spectrum and flexibility to implement their present and future communications needs.[24]

The U.S. Department of State tried to persuade the ITU nations to adopt the generic mobile satellite services spectrum allocation the United States had adopted domestically. There was, however, strong opposition to MSS allocations, especially from the Europeans who feared that it would adversely affect INMARSAT. Eventually, the United States was able to get a small LMSS allocation. WARC MOB-87 represented a compromise between those who wanted more spectrum allocated for MSS and those who sought to preserve the scarce mobile frequency spectrum for maritime and aeronautical users. Because the allocation was less than the United States wanted and probably less than what was needed to make the service economically viable, the United States took reservations on the land mobile allocations. The reservation essentially stipulated that the United States intended to continue its domestic allocation in spite of the decision agreed on by the conference participants.[25] Whether U.S. mobile services will be viable in the absence of protection from the international community remains an open question. The basic concern is that without international enforcement of the U.S. domestic allocation plan there may be great confusion and lack of coordination. The Air Transport Administration

(ATA), among others, argues that under existing ITU procedures, AMSC must accord priority to aeronautical services from other networks, not just aeronautical services on its own network. More generally, it maintains that because AMSC's L-band use does not conform with the international allocation of the band stipulated at WARC MOB-87, AMSC will not be able to coordinate its network under ITU procedures. Furthermore, ATA; Aeronautical Radio, Inc.; and COMSAT, the U.S. signatory to INTELSAT and INMARSAT, claim that AMSC will not be able to protect any LMSS traffic on frequencies the ITU has allocated to aeronautical use because other administrations are not required to protect nonconforming uses.[26]

THE EUROPEAN UNION

Although a description of the laws and regulations that govern satellite communications in Europe is beyond the scope of this chapter, a brief mention is in order with regard to some recent, significant trends.

As stated earlier, the European Union (EU) is taking on a larger role in the field of telecommunications. It has introduced measures to liberalize the supply of telecommunications equipment and services by enacting regulations known as directives. A directive is addressed to member states and requires them to achieve a specific result. Although it is binding as to the result to be achieved, it leaves discretion to national governments as to the form and method used to achieve that result.[27]

The two most important measures so far introduced by the EU are the Commission Directive on competition in the market of telecommunications terminal equipment[28] and the Commission Directive on competition in the markets for telecommunications.[29] Only the first directive applies to satellites for telecommunications and then only to satellite receive-only earth stations and not to other satellite terminal equipment as very small aperture terminal (VSAT). The commission of the EU has taken the first steps toward the liberalization of satellite communications on a community-wide basis. In November 1990, it published a document entitled "Towards Europe-wide Systems and Services: a Paper on a Common approach in the Field of Satellite Communications in the European Community." This document proposes four major changes:

1. full liberalization of the earth segment, including receive-only and transmit-receive terminals, subject to the necessary approval and licensing procedures;
2. unrestricted access to space segment capacity, subject to licensing procedures in order to safeguard those exclusive or special rights and regulatory provisions

set up by member states in conformity with EEC law: access to be on an equitable, nondiscriminatory, cost oriented basis;

3. full commercial freedom for space segment providers, including direct marketing of satellite capacity to service providers and users, subject to the above mentioned licensing procedures; and
4. harmonization measures as necessary to facilitate the provision of Europe-wide services, in particular, mutual recognition of licensing and type approval procedures, frequency coordination with regard to third country providers.[30]

The potential impact of the commission's proposals on international satellite organizations is controversial. There appear to be negotiations between the commission and EUTELSAT as to whether the changes proposed by the Commission can be achieved without amendment to the *EUTELSAT Convention* and *Operating Agreement*. The commission has also issued "Guidelines on the application of EEC competition rules in the telecommunications sector."[31] The guidelines raise two important points. The first is a statement that EU competition rules fully apply to satellites.[32] The second is the indication that agreements between European telecommunications organizations concerning the operation of satellite systems may be governed by EU antitrust rules.[33]

"Television without Frontiers" is another Community Directive intended to ensure that all broadcasts in the EEC are subject to the licensing controls of a member state when broadcast under its jurisdiction or when they make use of a frequency or satellite capacity granted by, or a satellite uplink in that member state. The practical meaning of that provision is that, for example, Belgium should exercise regulatory power over a Belgian company transmitting a satellite broadcast service for reception in France; or over a French company broadcasting service via an uplink in Belgium.[34]

THE UNITED KINGDOM[35]

The field of satellite communications in the United Kingdom is mostly regulated by four sets of laws. First, there is the regime established by the *Outer Space Act* of 1986, which provides for the licensing of aerospace activities, including the launching and operation of space objects. Then there is the law relating to telecommunications, to be found mostly in the *Telecommunications Act* of 1984. Third, there is the law relating to broadcasting, now to be found in the *Broadcasting Act* of 1990. Lastly, radio transmissions are regulated under the *Wireless Telegraphy Act* of 1949. These pieces of legislation apply to the entire territory of the United Kingdom. They operate in parallel so that individual licenses are required for broadcasting, launching a satellite and other relevant activities. The United Kingdom is also a party to all of the space treaties concluded under the auspices of the United Nations. The UK is a member of ITU, INTELSAT, INMARSAT, and EUTELSAT as well as a member of the European Economic Community, which exercises increasing influence in the regulation of telecommunications and broadcasting.

The long title of the Outer Space Act of 1986 is as follows: "*An Act to confer licensing and other powers on the Secretary of State to secure compliance with the international obligations of the United Kingdom with respect to the launching and operation of space objects and the carrying on of other activities in outer space by persons connected with this country.*" Accordingly, the act provides in Section 3 that a person to whom the act applies shall not carry on an activity regulated by the act except under the authority of a license granted by the secretary of state. The activities covered by the act are listed in Section 1 and are (1) launching or procuring the launch of a space object, (2) operating a space object, and (3) any activity in outer space. Of the three paragraphs, the more problematical would seem to be the second. It appears to apply to the operation of a satellite tracking, telemetry, and command (TT&C) station. It would also seem to apply to the operation of a TT&C station from a remote control center. It is not clear, however, whether it applies to operational decisions as opposed to mere implementation of those decisions. For example, it is doubtful whether a person who can decide to relocate a satellite or shut down a transponder is "operating" a space object, even though he can only implement his decisions by giving directions to a TT&C operator. It is also unclear whether operating a space object includes operating communications payload by controlling the allocation of communication channels.

Section 2 of the act provides that it applies to UK nationals, Scottish firms, and entities incorporated under the laws of any part of the United Kingdom. The act can be extended by Order in Council to entities incorporated under the law of any of the Channel Islands, the Isle of Man, or any dependent territory. This power has been exercised in relation to Guernsey, Hong Kong, the Isle of Man, and Jersey. Unlike the U.S. *Launch Act*, which applies to any launch within the U.S. territory, the British *Outer Space Act* does not apply to the launch of a space object by a foreign national, even from the territory of the UK.

Of more specific concern to satellite communications is the *Telecommunications Act of 1984*, which regulates the licensing of telecommunication systems. Section 4(1) defines telecommunication system as follows:

a system for the conveyance, through the agency of electric, magnetic, electro-magnetic, electro-chemical or electro-mechanical energy, of

a. speech, music and other sounds;
b. visual images;
c. signals serving for the impartation . . . of any matter otherwise than in the form of sounds or visual images; or
d. signals serving for the actuation or control of machinery or apparatus.

Section 4(2) extends the definition as follows:

For the purpose of this Act, telecommunication apparatus which is situated in the United Kingdom and

a. is connected to but not comprised in a telecommunication system; or
b. is connected to and comprised in a telecommunication system which extends beyond the United Kingdom,

shall be regarded as a telecommunication system and any person who controls the apparatus shall be regarded as running the system.

It follows from this language of the act that the operation of any satellite earth station in the United Kingdom will require a license, whether or not the station is connected to public networks, and regardless of whether communications with that station originate or terminate outside the UK.

The licensing power under the act is conferred on the secretary of state for trade and industry who must consult with the director general for telecommunications, who heads the regulatory body Office of Telecommunication (OFTEL).

It used to be that the Post Office had a monopoly over telecommunication networks, service, and equipment. Eventually, British Telecommunications (BT) took over the telecommunications business of the Post Office. In 1982, Mercury Communications Ltd., a competing public telecommunications operator, was licensed and, in 1984, BT was privatized. The British government made it clear that it did not intend to license any other entity, and a "duopoly" was thus created. In 1990 a review of that policy, known as the "Duopoly Review," began. As a result of that consultation process the government issued a White Paper in March 1991 called "Competition and Choice: Telecommunications Policy of the 1990's,"[36] which, in effect, ended the Duopoly Policy. It announced that it would consider any application for a license to offer telecommunication services over fixed links within the UK.

Although this change of policy may herald the arrival of new competition for BT and Mercury, the position of satellite service is complicated. The White Paper announced that it intended to issue a class license that would authorize provision of satellite services through systems that are not connected to the public switched network at either end. A class license granted in 1991 permits the provision of any telecommunications service consisting in the transmission of messages to or the reception of messages from earth orbiting apparatus that permits a wide range of services: one-way or two-way, point-to-point or to multi-point, domestic or international. There are, however, two exceptions. The first is that the transmission and reception of messages are to be conveyed by means of a public telecommunications system. The second exception is the television and sound broadcasts for subsequent delivery to groups of dwellings, a reference to satellite-to-cable systems, which are licensed under the *Broadcasting Act* of 1990.

Note that the use of a class license for receive or transmit earth stations, whether fixed or mobile, provides a framework not only for the use of VSAT services in the United Kingdom but also for the development of land mobile-satellite services. The new class license is in direct competition with the former Duopoly but the government remains cautious with respect to satellite services interconnecting with the public switched network. The White Paper states that such services will need to be considered on a case-by-case basis. The White Paper, in essence, leaves the door open to operators wishing to provide domestic satellite services connected to the public switched network. With regard to international switched services via satellite, the paper makes reference to criteria proposed elsewhere in the document, leaving little hope for the time being for new operators to offer services in competition with BT and Mercury. The government is reluctant to license any new international operators, whatever transmission medium they may use. Among the reasons for that hesitation is the fear that foreign monopoly administrations may take advantage of British operators and that British operators will not find overseas the same kind of competitive environment proposed in the UK.

Potential satellite service providers still have some possibilities. Under a class license known as the Branch Systems General License, a service provider can resell capacity on BT or Mercury international private leased circuits. There is also a license available for self-provided telecommunication systems under which a person may run a system for his own purposes. It is now also possible to effect an international simple resale of private leased circuits. "Simple resale" is intended to be the resale of capacity in international private circuits that are connected to the private switch networks at both ends. The director general of telecommunications has recently advised the secretary of state that international simple resale should be permitted but only where equal liberalization has taken place in the other country concerned.[37]

An issue still unresolved is access to the space segment, which could effectively curb competition. As a signatory to INTELSAT, EUTELSAT, and INMARSAT, for example, BT is not required under its license to offer services using those space segments. The class license for satellite services authorizes the connection of stations to any satellite provided that the relevant requirements for consultation under the rules of those organizations have been satisfied. Operators wishing to use the INTELSAT, INMARSAT or EUTELSAT space segments in providing service will have to obtain space segment capacity through BT, even though they may be using such space segments under their own licenses. This situation is brought about by Article XV of the INTELSAT Operating Agreement, which requires that any application for allotment of INTELSAT space segment be submitted by a signatory of INTELSAT. EUTELSAT and INMARSAT have corresponding provisions. The anticompetitive effects of this legal framework follow from the fact that a satellite service provider has to obtain space segment capacity through BT. Because BT already has a dominant position in the market, satellite service operators would stand to lose a great deal by having to disclose their commercial information and business plans to BT, their potential competitor.

Satellite broadcasting in the United Kingdom is governed by the *Broadcasting Act* of 1990. The act provides for the licensing of three categories of broadcasting service. The first is the "domestic satellite system." The second is the "non-domestic satellite service," which has a two-part definition:

1. a service that consists in the transmission of television programs by satellite (a) otherwise than on an allocated frequency, and (b) for general reception in the United Kingdom or in any prescribed country (or both), where the programs are transmitted from UK territory; or
2. a service that consists in the transmission of television programs by satellites (a) from a place that is neither in the United Kingdom nor in any prescribed country, but (b) for such reception as is mentioned in paragraph 1(b), if and to the extent that the programs included in it consist of material to be provided by a person in the United Kingdom who is in a position to determine what is to be included in the service.[38]

The first part of this definition in effect provides that a service may be up-linked from the United Kingdom and intended for general reception there, but will nevertheless be classified as a "non-domestic satellite service" if it is transmitted other than on an allocated frequency. Part two of the definition, on the other hand, ensures that a satellite program service which is effectively controlled from the UK and intended for general reception there does not avoid British licensing controls solely because a signal is up-linked from another country. The reference to "any prescribed country" in the definition enables the UK to implement its obligations under the previously mentioned European Community Directive Television Without Frontiers. An order has now been made under the *Broadcasting Act* that defines all the other countries of the EU as "prescribed countries." Pursuant to this list, the definition of "non-domestic satellite service" in the act becomes consistent with the directive. Part one of the definition now covers any service up-linked from the UK and intended for general reception in the UK or any other EU country or both. Part two refers to any service up-linked from a place outside the EU but intended for reception in the UK or any other EU country or both, provided that the program content is substantially determined by a person in the United Kingdom. Neither part of the definition covers a service that is linked from another European Union (EU) country but that is intended for reception in the UK.[39]

NOTES

1. See John Davidson Thomas, *International Aspects of the Mobile Satellite Services*, 43 Federal Communications Law Journal, 1991, at 46.
2. 47 U.S.C. § 307(a) (1989).
3. See Karl-Heinz Neumann, *Toward a Market-Driven Frequency Management Policy*, Satellite Communications, January 1992, p. 26.
4. Released on September 29, 1992, to revise Report No. DS-1202 7 FCC Red 3600 (1992).
5. 47 C.F.R. § 1.1307 (Question No. 25, FCC Form 493).
6. 47 C.F.R. § 304.
7. 50 FR 42266 (October 18, 1985), 101 FCC 2d 1046 (1985).
8. See Lou Manuta, *Playing the Game*, Satellite Communications, July 1992, p. 14.
9. *Id.*, at 16.
10. *Id.*, at 17.
11. *Id.*, at 19.
12. *Id.*, at 19.
13. See Lou Manuta, *Influencing the Process*, Satellite Communications, August 1992, p. 31.
14. *Id.*
15. *Id.*
16. *Id.*, at 32.
17. See Nordwall, *Mobile Satellite Firms Expect Strong Market Growth in 1990*, Aviation Week and Space Technology, December 19, 1988 at 89, in Davidson Thomas, *supra*, at note 5.

18. 50 Fed. Reg. 8, 149 (1985).

19. *Id.*, at 8, 155–166.

20. See Thomas, *supra*, at p. 50.

21. Amendment of Parts 2, 22 and 25 of the Commission's Rules to Allocate Spectrum for and to Establish Other Rules and Policies Pertaining to the Use of Radio Frequencies in a Mobile Satellite Service for the Provision of Various Common Carrier Services, 4 FCC Rcd 6016, 1018, 66 R.R. 2nd. 1351, 1356 (1989).

22. Among the eight applicants that comprise the AMSC are Hughes Communications Mobile Satellite, Inc., American Satellite Service Corporation, McCaw Space Technologies, American Mobile Satellite, Inc., Transit Communications, Inc., Satellite Mobile Telephone Co., and Skylink Corporation.

23. Davidson Thomas, *supra*, at p. 51.

24. See Davidson Thomas, *supra*, p. 55, note 27.

25. *Id.*, at p. 58.

26. *Id.*, p. 59.

27. See Philip Dann, *Law and Regulation of Satellite Communications in the United Kingdom*, 20 Journal of Space Law 1, 1992, p. 15.

28. Commission Directive 88/301/EEC of May 16, 1988.

29. Commission Directive 90/388/EEC of June 28, 1990.

30. See Dann, *supra*, at 16.

31. Official Journal of the European Communities 91/C 233/02.

32. *Id.*, § 124.

33. *Id.*, § 126.

34. See Article 2(1) of the directive.

35. This section of the chapter is, in part, a summary of Dann, *supra*.

36. Dept. of Trade and Industry, Cm 1461 (1990).

37. OFTEL NEWS, October 1990, p. 1.

38. Broadcasting Act 1990, § 43(2).

39. See Dann, *supra*, at 20.

Chapter Six

Financing

For many years, aerospace activities have been undertaken by governments and a few large contractors. As the technology evolved and the field of space activities grew in the past decade or so, a private sector is emerging that involves all the traditional elements of private enterprise. Good prospects for effective and lucrative access to space have awakened the interest of the business community and spawned dozens of new private ventures, all of which need funding to get started and operate. Among the successfully commercialized space ventures are communications satellites, launch services, remote sensing, payload processing, space-based facilities, manufacturing, materials processing, support facilities, and others.

SOURCES AND METHODS OF FINANCING

If funding is what makes commercial space ventures possible, it also raises a broad range of legal issues. It requires expertise in space law, government contracts, securities law, corporations, and other related fields. It is a particularly complex type of financing because of the unique nature of aerospace activities, which can best be described by identifying the characteristics that those activities have in common.

Aerospace projects require enormous amounts of capital. Development costs can run $50 million or more, whereas space ventures can exceed $200 million.[1] Although, in the case of a pioneering company, high start-up costs may sometimes be offset by barriers to competitive entries by others, subsequent entrants would have a smaller market and a less favorable financial return projection.

Space ventures often require a longer time span for financial returns to materialize. Three or more years may pass from a project's initial concept to launch and several more may be needed for a return on the investment. For the project's return to be competitive with other investment opportunities, the profits must be substantially greater.[2] There is also, in space ventures, a high level of actual or perceived risk. The actual risk is related to uncertainties as to whether it will work, the price at which it will sell, the time it will take, and the emergence of unforseen problems. Those risk factors can only be compensated by the prospect of high return or exceptional growth potential. A Standard and Poor type rating for space projects will be available only after substantial experience establishes the credibility of project risk assessments in the field.[3]

The glamor of space projects may attract early-stage investors who provide seed capital but adequate multistage financing is unlikely in the absence of serious education of investors on space technology and business prospects. What detracts from the appeal of space ventures is the unpredictability of technical factors as well as the relative novelty of the market.

Another element shared by most aerospace activities is the high level of technology required. To better handle the formidable scientific and technical challenges, space projects draw on an outstanding pool of managerial and technical talent. It is the caliber of a project's team that often determines investment decisions.

There are many special factors affecting financing in the aerospace field, which must be carefully examined. Is a project feasible from a technical standpoint, and can it be done within the time and cost estimate? If, for example, the operation involves the space shuttle or the space station, will the project meet the interface and safety requirements that might be imposed by the National Aeronautics and Space Administration? Is the market sufficient to provide a return on the investment and how will the market be when the project is completed, or later if there are delays?[4] The ability to obtain financing obviously depends on the extent of competition. A typical question is whether the product is unique and whether it can be duplicated by applying ground-based technology.

When the government is a consumer of the product of a space venture, financing presents special considerations. Investment bankers and commercial banks do not consider the government a very reliable customer. Reasons for the uncertainties involved in dealing with the government include the Office of Management and Budget process, the appropriation and authorization process, and the changing nature of many government programs. The government may also terminate a contract for convenience, which leaves a private company without profits. Unfortunately for the company seeking funds, when the government is the principal customer, it usually requires funding to award the contract and the lender requires the contract in order to provide financing.[5]

Another issue to be considered is whether all the licenses and permits have been obtained. The Department of Transportation, Office of Commercial Space Transportation (OCST) must issue a license for a launch; the Department of Commerce's approval is required for remote sensing activities; the Federal Communications Commission must approve any lunch of communications satellites; and NASA or other agencies may have to agree to the use of government facilities. If the contract is classified by the Department of Defense or another agency, a whole set of requirements takes effect.

Most space ventures also have to deal with insurance questions, which can be quite complex and modify the financial parameters of a given operation. As explained in detail in the insurance chapter, there are several types of insurance that are specific to commercial space ventures. They include prelaunch insurance, space flight insurance, credit enhancement insurance, and flight delay insurance. Ordinary types of insurance are also applicable, such as property and casualty insurance; general liability; employers, officers, and directors liability; and others.

The sources of financing can be many. Personal assets of the organizers often serve as seed capital, as can those of the friends and relatives of the organizers. Those who hold a stake in the venture can be another source of funding. These stakeholders are those who have a particular interest in the success of a venture or are making some contribution to the company, such as manufacturing a facility or being a sales agent. They include suppliers and subcontractors of the space project. Their participation may be through debt, equity, or by way of a joint venture. Other sources of funding are venture capital firms, direct investment institutions such as insurance companies, private placements, investment bankers, commercial banks, and public offerings.

David Thompson of Orbital Sciences Corporation lists four basic types of financing: equity financing, debt capitalization, internal funds generation, and innovative financing. Equity is basically the exchange of stock in a company for capital. Equity financing is most frequently used in the start-up phase of an enterprise and in early and further development stages. Debt may take the form of short-term loans from banks or intermediate- to long-term notes from other lenders such as savings associations and small business investment companies. This type of capitalization may be available if the creditworthiness of a space project can be assured or if tangible assets are available as collateral and provide secured financing. Because principal and interest payments are often tailored to the cash flow of the venture, this type of financing is usually not available in the initial stages of the project. In the case of large enterprises with sustained profitability, internal funds or revenue may be available for reinvestment in new space projects. By its very nature, this type of funding is not available to capitalize new ventures. Innovative financing techniques include research and development limited partnerships (RDLP) and debt-equity hybrid instruments. The limited partnership may raise capital in amounts much greater than usually available from equity sources, making them attractive to start-up and small ventures. A properly structured RDLP also offers tax and other advantages.

In the early stages of a space project it is advisable to keep the financial structure as simple as possible. Once the venture is operating successfully with a proven product, it may wish to make its initial private offering. This phase should be the last stage for a project after it has utilized all the private markets available.[6]

Certain forms of governmental financial assistance are often necessary for new space ventures. The various support mechanisms include new technology procurement, demonstration projects, low-cost payload integration services, free or low-cost shuttle flights for in-flight payloads and transportation to a space station or platform, as well as readily available information on new technologies. The government could also assist American companies in meeting foreign competition and promoting exports. Such assistance could take the form of subsidized financing, cross-border tax leases, and counter-trades or offsets. Subsidized financing could involve loan guarantees at commercial rates for foreign purchases to lower the effective costs of space hardware and launch services. Cross-border tax leases could also lower export prices. As they have with commercial aircraft export, U.S. taxpayers reduce their taxes through depreciation and investment tax credits while leasing equipment to foreign users. Counter-trades and offsets are requirements to purchase exports from or make technological investments in purchasing countries.[7]

Very large projects are often undertaken with international financial participation. This could take the form of financing from official sources such as loans at concessionary rates for medium or long terms, multilateral agency funds, bilateral aid, and contributions in kind.[8]

SECURED FINANCING

Lending to creditworthy entities for lucrative ventures is the primary object and business of institutional lenders and venture capitalists alike. The problem, however, is that in the field of aerospace activities, in addition to the many uncertainties mentioned above, it is particularly difficult to secure certain assets, which must serve as collateral for various types of loans. Although commercial activities in space have greatly expanded, the applicable laws lag far behind.

Secured transactions have long been an invaluable tool to finance small or risky businesses, particularly in the first, difficult stages. Article 9 of the *Uniform Commercial Code* (UCC) is one of the cardinal principles of U.S. law on secured transactions. The application of the code extends beyond lending transactions to include leases and consignments.[9] Just as asset-based financing was used in the aviation industry, aerospace companies are using sale-leaseback arrangements and obtaining loans to finance the equipment placed into earth orbit. The code, however, does not take into consideration the unique problems presented by assets located in space.

Article II of the 1967 *Treaty on Principles Governing the Activities of States in the Exploration and Use of Outer Space, Including the Moon and Other Celestial Bodies*, commonly known as the Outer Space Treaty, provides that "outer space, including the Moon and other celestial bodies, is not subject to national appropriation by means of use or occupation, or by any other means." By prohibiting the assertion of national territorial claims in outer space, the article deprives states of the right to extend their jurisdiction and control over any part of space. Article II also provides that "exploration and use of outer space . . . shall be the province of all mankind." As a signatory to that treaty, the United States has renounced the right of states to exert sovereignty over any part of space.

Private activities in space have not been prohibited by international law and private companies are free to participate in space development provided, of course, that they abide by the relevant provisions of national and international law.

Article VIII of the Outer Space Treaty provides that "ownership of objects launched into outer space, including objects landed or constructed on a celestial body, and their component parts, is not affected by their presence in outer space or on a celestial body or by their return to the Earth." The issue of property rights in space becomes more complicated with regard to objects found naturally in space. It is not clear whether natural resources in space can be appropriated by a state or private entities. That question is also underscored by the language of the 1979 *Agreement Governing the Activities of States on the Moon and Other Celestial Bodies* (the Moon Treaty), which provides that natural resources in space are the "common heritage of mankind." It is likely that property rights in celestial bodies and their minerals will eventually become subject to a complex international legal system.[10]

Article 9 of the UCC restricts its coverage to the creation of security interests in "personal property or fixtures" and expressly excludes the "creation or transfer of an interest in or lien in real estate." It would therefore appear that Article 9 coverage of "personal property" would extend to all interests in spaceborne property. It is not clear, however, what the status would be of those objects attached to the surface of the Moon or another planet. Although those objects would be in constant motion relative to earth, in a physical sense they would form part of or be the local real estate of that planet.

International space law clearly establishes that celestial bodies are neither subject nor susceptible to the property laws of individual nations. Article 9 of the code provides that personal property includes "goods," which it defines, in part, as "all things which are movable at the time the security interest attaches." This definition would include objects manufactured or artificially placed in outer space. Goods, however, are expressly defined as not to include "minerals or the like . . . before extraction." The concept of celestial real estate would encompass naturally occurring mineral aggregates such as asteroids and planetoids before they have been reduced to possession.[11]

Even assuming that Article 9 of the code covers spaceborne collateral property, that is only one of the issues presented by secured financing for space activities. A secured lender would want to know that the UCC is in fact applicable. Under certain circumstances, long-arm statutes provide for the extension of a states's jurisdiction beyond its borders. Under international law, a sovereign state has authority to exercise its jurisdiction over matters outside its territory provided this exercise is not unreasonable. The *Reinstatement of Foreign Relations* (Second) provides that reasonableness is determined by a consideration of numerous relevant factors, including the relative interests of other states, potential conflict with other states' regulations, traditions of the international system, and the connections with and the importance to the state exercising jurisdiction.[12] A state may thus regulate matters that have a substantial effect within its territory, the conduct of interests of the nation outside its territory, and persons or things aboard a vessel or aircraft registered in that state. In fact, vessels and aircraft are even said to have the nationality of the state of registry and are subject to the state's authority, enforcement, and judicial jurisdiction.

Article VIII of the *Outer Space Treaty* provides that "a State Party to the Treaty on whose registry an object launched into outer space is carried shall retain jurisdiction and control over such object, and over any personnel thereof, while in outer space or on a celestial body." That article seems to establish that international law recognizes the authority of the United States to exercise jurisdiction over spaceborne objects on its registry. The terms "launched into outer space," however, may not encompass objects originated in space that are not in the registry of the United States. A nation's jurisdiction over objects that are not covered by the article would have to be inferred from a number of other factors such as the nationality of the object's owner, the site of the launch, and all other elements of ownership.

Even if U.S. jurisdiction can be established, it remains to be seen whether individual states within the United States can apply their commercial codes to spaceborne property. International law concerns itself only with the scope of state jurisdiction and not with the allocation of that jurisdiction within a federal state. Federal authority to regulate spaceborne objects might readily be derived from the federal government's power to regulate foreign relations or interstate and foreign commerce. Although state regulation of rights in spaceborne objects cannot be said to have been preempted by Congress, it is possible that such regulation would constitute an intrusion into an exclusively federal domain.[13] Unless, however, there is potential for conflict with international agreements or state actions overstep limits clearly set for U.S. discretion, federal authority in foreign relations should not prevent commercial laws of individual states from regulating rights in spaceborne objects under U.S. jurisdiction.

Even though laws of individual states of the United States may govern certain property and secured rights over spaceborne property, state courts in general cannot exercise attachment jurisdiction over property located outside the forum state because attachment and sequestration depend on the levying of process by state officials whose authority extends only to state boundaries. Nevertheless, a state court may compel persons over whom it has jurisdiction to convey their interests in foreign land to others, as it may order a debtor to bring personal property within its control to the state for attachment.[14] There is, therefore, little doubt that a state court can adjudicate the relative rights of persons in spaceborne property provided it has personal jurisdiction over those persons.

The UCC provides certain choice of law rules that state courts must observe when adjudicating with respect to code transactions. Section 1–105 permits the parties to choose the law governing their transaction, provided the transaction bears a reasonable relation to the chosen state. The code provides in Section 9–103(1) that perfection of security interests in documents of title, negotiable instruments, and goods that are not minerals nor mobile goods, nor covered by a certificate of title, is governed by "the law of the jurisdiction where the collateral is when the last event occurs on which is based the assertion that the security interest is perfected or unperfected."

According to the second restatement, general conflict-of-law principles provide that the validity and effect of a security interest in personal property are determined by the state having the "most significant relationship" to the parties, the property, and the security interest. Selection of law by agreement between the parties will be given considerable if not decisive weight. Uncertainty could be minimized by agreement in advance on the state whose law should govern through Section 9–103(1) while the collateral remains in space. In the absence of an effective choice of law by the parties, courts would normally give predominant consideration to the collateral's location at the time of attachment.[15] Personal property in space, however, has no physical contact with any state and spaceborne collateral could then be treated as the "general intangibles" of Section 9–103(3) of the code, which requires that interests be perfected under the laws of the jurisdiction where the debtor is located. When the debtor moves to another jurisdiction, the secured party would have four months to perfect its security interest under the laws of the new state. The most prudent course of action for a secured party, however, would probably be to perform a lien search and perfect its security interest in every state that might have the requisite minimum contacts with the debtor, the collateral, and the secured party. It would also be a good idea to monitor the debtor's activities in other states to clearly assess its priority.[16]

Section 9–103(3) of the UCC provides that "the law of the jurisdiction where the debtor is located" governs perfection and of security interests in "goods which are mobile and which are of a type normally used in more than one jurisdiction." Under this provision, goods must be analogous to motor vehicles, trailers, airplanes, and such. In a physical sense, satellites and other objects in space can be considered mobile in the sense that they are in constant motion in relation to the earth. It is doubtful, however, whether they meet the criteria of Section 9–103(3) because they do not pass from one state jurisdiction to another, as is the case with rolling stock, trailers, and other vehicles. Furthermore, Section 9–103(3) applies to mobile goods only if they constitute "inventory leased or held for lease by the debtor to others" or equipment. This excludes inventory used in the debtor's operations or held by the debtor for sale, which could be very important for manufacturing companies in asset-based financing. It is reasonable to conclude that Section 9–103(3) of the code does not govern the vast majority of spaceborne property.

For what concerns minerals, UCC Section 9–103(5) provides that perfection of a security interest in minerals that attaches on extraction is governed by the law of the jurisdiction in which the mine or wellhead is located. In the case of minerals located in outer space, the applicable law could be the international law governing outer space. Such law, however, does not yet provide a system for perfecting security interests.

Once a state has been identified whose laws may govern perfection of its security interests, the secured party should perfect under those laws. Section 9–401 of the code provides the details for the filing.

In conclusion, it can be said that a careful planning of the secured transaction can go a long way toward reducing the problems, confusion, and dangers, for the party to be secured. In particular, the parties should agree to the following terms.

1. *Jurisdiction over the space object.* The collateral should remain located in an area where the United States can assert jurisdiction and control under the Outer Space Treaty. To avoid any ambiguities and complications the following guidelines should be followed:

a. the collateral should be launched from a territory belonging to the United States or a nation with whom an agreement exists for U.S. control of the launch;

b. the launching entity should be a person or entity having U.S. nationality;

c. the debtor should be a person or business entity organized under the laws of the United States with its principal office in a state of the United States that has adopted the UCC;

d. the object should be registered with the United States, and its registry should be properly reported to the United Nations in accordance with the Registration Convention; and

e. the collateral or the object containing it should not be joined to another object subject to the jurisdiction of another nation.

If it is not possible to secure U.S. jurisdiction as just suggested, a new analysis should then be undertaken of the laws and regulations of the country that is believed likely to obtain jurisdiction, and then perfect any secured rights according to the laws of that country.[17]

2. *Debtor's worldwide contacts.* The debtor should disclose the nature and extent of its activities in other states for a reasonable period preceding the proposed transaction. The reason for this precaution is to identify possible states that may later be invoked as having jurisdiction over the collateral. The secured party should then perfect its interest under the laws of any state with significant contacts.

3. *Conditions for return to earth.* The collateral should not be returned to earth without the secured party having consented to it or having received timely notice. This will give the secured party sufficient opportunity to

determine the applicability of the laws of any state where the collateral is to be removed.

4. *Remedies for default.* The security agreement should contain language to incorporate Section 9–503 of the code that enables the secured party to require the debtor to assemble the collateral and make it available to the secured party. It should also grant the secured party the right to sell the collateral without removal, as provided by Section 9–504.[18]

The particular provisions suggested above are, of course, in addition to and not in lieu of the normal conditions used in ordinary secured transactions agreements.

NOTES

1. Edward Ridley Finch, Jr., and Amanda Lee Moore, *Astrobusiness: A Guide to the Commerce and Law of Outer Space*, Praeger Publishers, New York, 1985, p. 48.
2. *Id.*
3. *Id.*, p. 49.
4. S. Neil Hosenball, *Financing Space Ventures*, 4 Journal of Law and Technology, 1989, p. 16.
5. *Id.*
6. See Finch and Moore, *supra*, p. 50.
7. *Id.*, pp. 53–54.
8. *Id.*
9. U.C.C. par. 1–201(37) defining "security interest" to include leases and consignments "intended as security."
10. See Richard D. Cunningham, *Space Commerce and Secured Financing—New Frontiers for the U.C.C.*, The Business Lawyer, May 1985, pp. 806 *et seq.*
11. *Id.*, at 811.
12. § 403(1).
13. *See* Cunningham, *supra*, at 816–817.
14. For a discussion of these principles, see Miller v. Miller, 109 Misc. 2nd. 982, 441 N.Y.S. 2d 339, 341 (N.Y. Sup. Ct. 1981); Shaffer v. Heitner, 433 U.S. at 211 n.38; also see Cunningham, *supra*, p. 821.
15. Restatement (Second) of Conflict of Laws par. 251 comment e, at 94 and 95 (1971).
16. See Cunningham, *supra*, p. 827.
17. *Id.*, at 831–832, and the notes thereto.
18. *Id.*

Chapter Seven

Space Transportation

Maritime, rail, road, and air transportation all presented technological challenges and risks and, initially, their regulation involved trial and error. Eventually, however, they assisted in stimulating economic growth and improving the quality of life. Although the commercial launch industry is at an early stage of development, its rate of growth is impressive and will require an extensive amount of national and international regulation.

It is important to distinguish private from government launch programs. Enormous capital requirements and national security considerations have traditionally restricted launch activities to the government. Although governments continue to play an essential role in space transportation today, the private sector is greatly increasing its share of the business.[1] With the growth of this new private industry comes a whole set of legal issues ranging from basic contract law to tort law, licensing, regulatory matters, and export controls.

INTERNATIONAL LAW

From the very beginning of the space age, the international community realized the need to develop a set of principles to govern activities in space. The first instrument of international regulation, or at least the attempt to regulate, can be traced to a resolution of the General Assembly of the United Nations of 1958 regarding the peaceful uses of outer space, the sovereign equality of all countries relating to space activities, and the need for international cooperation.[2] The United Nations also established in 1958 an ad hoc Committee on the Peaceful Uses of Outer Space (COPUOS), which eventually became the most important United Nations body dealing with space activities. There are several other space-related organizations, but no international organization has been created expressly to assume responsibility for space transportation.

COPUOS, with the help of its Legal Subcommittee, has given direction to the development of several space treaties. The first of these agreements was the *Treaty on Principles Governing the Activities of States in the Exploration and Use of Outer Space, Including the Moon and Other Celestial Bodies*, which was opened for signature on January 27, 1967. That agreement, commonly referred to as the Outer Space Treaty, is considered the basic legal instrument from which all other treaties on space activities were derived. In 1968, another treaty was completed, the *Agreement on the Rescue of Astronauts, The Return of Astronauts and The Return of Objects Launched into Outer Space*, also known as the Rescue Agreement. In 1972 a very important instrument was concluded, the *Convention on International Liability for Damage Caused by Space Objects*, commonly known as the Liability Convention. A 1976 agreement, the *Convention on Registration of Objects Launched in Outer Space*, or the Registration Convention, instituted an international registry of all objects launched into the earth's orbit. The 1979 Moon Treaty, officially the *Agreement Governing the Activities of States on the Moon and Other Celestial Bodies*, contained more ideological and controversial principles.

These agreements are of a general nature and have been supplemented by more detailed regulations in various fields, such as remote sensing, satellite communications, and direct television broadcasting. Space transportation, however, has not been directly regulated yet and even the space treaties are not clearly applicable. For example, the term "spacecraft" or "space vehicle" is not used in any of the space agreements, which use instead the more general "space object."[3] If the term "space object" is broad enough to encompass spacecraft such as the Space Shuttle, space transportation would be subject to the registration requirements under the Registration Convention and liability obligations under the Liability Convention.

The most important provision that can be considered applicable to space transportation is article VI of the Outer Space Treaty.[4] That article provides that a state must be responsible for national space activities and shall require "authorization" and exercise "continuing supervision" of private entities. Article VIII is also important in that it provides that the state of registry of an object launched into outer space "shall retain jurisdiction and control over such object, and over any personnel thereof." There seems to be little doubt that space transportation activities fall within the scope of those provisions. The concepts of "authorization," "state responsibility," "continuing supervision," and "jurisdiction and control," however, are not specific enough to create clear legal requirements. Article VI, for example, does not explicitly delineate the exact nature of commercial entities' right to engage in space transportation, nor the corresponding obligations of states to oversee and regulate this activity. It follows that states can regulate space transportation activities in accordance with the general requirements of Article VI without coordinating their national regulations with other states. The international agreements on space activities can, therefore, be said to leave most regulation of space transportation to the discretion of individual states.

U.S. LAW

For more than 30 years, all U.S. space activities were conducted by the federal government. During that time, expendable launch vehicles with a range of lift capabilities were developed to carry out suborbital, orbital, and planetary missions. Combined efforts of the military, scientific, and industrial space communities produced a tremendous growth in the American launch technology. Today, the U.S. commercial space transportation industry is composed of a variety of companies, including major, established aerospace firms and smaller entrepreneurial businesses. These companies provide launch services to a wide range of domestic and foreign customers as well as the U.S. government.

The *National Aeronautics and Space Act* of 1958[5] designates NASA as the main agency responsible for the direction of U.S. aeronautical and space research programs and related activities. It also provides authority for NASA to operate the space transportation system, that is the Space Shuttle, on a routine basis. Until the enactment of the *Commercial Space Launch Act* of 1984,[6] the regulation of private space transportation in the United States was fragmentary and inconsistent. A launch by a private entity would require a waiver of applicable Federal Aviation Administration (FAA) Regulations governing suborbital rocket launches. Radio licenses would have to be obtained by the Federal Communications Commission, and the Department of State would have to grant the licenses required by the *Export Control Act*. NASA would also be involved in reviewing the technical safety of a launch. An example of the procedures involved in launch activities until 1984 was given by the application for launch permission in 1981 by Space Services, Inc., of America. As part of the launch permission process, Space Services obtained a waiver of applicable FAA regulations for the launch of unmanned rockets.[7] As a condition to granting the waiver, the FAA required that the rocket land within U.S. territorial waters.[8] Following a launch accident, Space Services launched, in September 1982, a new rocket that traveled over 300 miles in ten minutes and landed in international waters. In spite of FAA and other agencies cooperation with Space Services, the company had to deal with many uncertainties. As outlined, launch permission was also subject to an experimental radio license granted by the FCC. Also, the Department of State had to issue an export license under the authority of the *Arms Export Control Act*. The reason for requiring an export license was to ensure compliance with international treaties concerning government liability for private space activity such as the Liability Convention.[9]

In 1983, the government issued a commercial directive that included encouragement of a private sector expendable launch vehicle capability, with key technology to be made available to industry at no cost, while federal launch capacity could be used on a direct cost reimbursement basis. Other supportive policy statements followed. They include the National Space Policy (1989), the Commercial Space Launch Policy (1990), the Commercial Space Policy Guidelines (1991), and the National Launch Strategy (1991). These statements reaffirmed the government's commitment to fostering commercial space activities. In 1984, the Department of Transportation (DOT) was designated as the lead agency for commercial launch activities. Later that year, Congress enacted the *Commercial Space Launch Act* of 1984, which authorized DOT to regulate U.S. commercial launch activities.[10] The Office of Commercial Space Transportation of DOT and its three divisions carry out DOT's dual responsibilities under the act, (1) to license and regulate all U.S. commercial launch activities and to ensure that they are conducted safely and responsibly and (2) to promote, encourage, and facilitate commercial space transportation.

Section 2605 of the Launch Act prohibits the launch of a launch vehicle or operation of a launch site by any person within the United States or by a U.S. citizen anywhere unless authorized by a license issued under the Act. Section 2603(6) defines "launch vehicle" as "any vehicle constructed for the purpose of operating in, or placing a payload in, outer space and any suborbital rocket." The definition does not include upper stages, probably with the intention of leaving upper stages, with their uncertain role and capabilities, to later consideration.[11]

Payloads aboard a launch vehicle are not under the jurisdiction of DOT. A launch license holder, however, must comply with all laws and regulations applicable to the payload before deployment. If a permit or license is required for the payload, the DOT need only ascertain that a license has been obtained. If a proposed payload is somehow not covered by a license, the DOT has the responsibility to assess the potential for harm to the public property, national security, or foreign policy interests of the United States and to prevent launch if necessary.[12] The act defines payload as "an object which a person undertakes to place in outer space by means of a launch vehicle specifically designed or adapted for that object."[13] Under this definition, the OCST has found only two types of payloads that are licensed by other agencies: telecommunications satellites by the Federal Communications Commission and remote sensing satellites by the Department of Commerce.[14] Payload might also include passengers or passenger modules. Because a passenger module would necessarily return to earth, it might constitute a re-entry vehicle meeting the *Federal Aviation Act*'s definition of an aircraft and thereby involve the licensing authority of the FAA. The Federal Aviation Administration issues airworthiness certificates pursuant to 49 U.S.C. app. 1424 and 14 C.F.R. pt. 3, and defines "aircraft" as "a device that is used or intended to be used for flight in the air." It is therefore possible that in the future the FAA may be called on to issue airworthiness certificates for payloads designed and intended to be used for flight in the air. The FAA, however, is unlikely to become involved in the regulation of combined space-aircraft vehicles as it did with the Space Shuttle, and regulation of passenger-carrying space-aircraft (such as the proposed National Space Plane) would be the responsibility of OCST.[15]

Launch sites are brought under DOT's control by Section 2606 of the act, and the OCST is now responsible for the licensing of all aspects of a private launch site except radio communications, which remain under the authority of the FCC. In compliance with Article VI of the Outer Space Treaty and relevant provisions of the Liability Convention, the act requires a launch license for all launches in U.S. territory or by U.S. citizens anywhere. A "United States citizen" includes all citizens, business entities organized in the United States, and foreign corporations controlled by U.S. citizens or business entities.[16]

As noted, the Office of Commercial Space Transportation is responsible for administering its regulatory authority to protect public health and safety, safety of property, the national security, and foreign policy interests of the United States, and to ensure compliance with U.S. international obligations. The OCST Licensing and Safety Division is responsible for a number of regulatory functions that are essential to ensure the safety of commercial space launch activities. Before a vehicle can be launched, the OCST must, therefore, issue a license. The license is a single-page document executed by the associate director for licensing programs and authorizes the licensee to conduct specified commercial space launch activities subject to the terms of the *Commercial Space Launch Act* and the orders, rules, and regulations issued thereunder. Licenses for single missions have attached two launch orders. Order "A" specifically states the type of space activities authorized (including the type of launch vehicle to be used, the launch site, and the payload) and certain obligations of the licensee, such as accident reporting, records to be maintained, and monitoring and compliance requirements. License order "B" establishes financial responsibility requirements for commercial space launch activities.[17]

Before the OCST will issue a license for an unmanned launch, the applicant must obtain mission and safety approval.[18] This twofold licensing process allows the government to effectively review its two major areas of concern and allows an applicant to receive approval of certain matters during the planning stages of a launch. A license contains the conditions an applicant must meet before launch. Failure to comply with those conditions would result in denial of the application.

The safety review process is designed to ensure that a proposed launch does not endanger public safety and it leads to "safety approval." If the vehicle is to be launched from a federally operated range or a site operated under an OCST-issued license, the safety review process is rather pro forma, and approval will be given when the proposed launch is accepted by a range or launch site capable of handling the operation. The only condition will be compliance with the range or site operation regulations. This presumption of safety operates under the assumption that federal or licensed sites conform to general standards for location, operation procedures, personnel qualifications, and equipment quality.[19]

When a launch is to take place from a site not already licensed, the safety process is rather complicated. The applicant must demonstrate that it possesses the capability and resources to safely conduct the preparation and launch of a launch vehicle and any accompanying payloads. Because launch site safety standards or requirements have not yet been developed, the OCST will treat each launch application on a case-by-case basis. The applicant is required to submit detailed information designed to ensure a safe site location, proper operation procedures, qualified personnel, and adequate equipment. The safety review process will also examine the payloads accompanying the launch vehicle. If the payload is a communication satellite or a remote sensing satellite, the OCST will initially determine whether a license has been issued by the FCC or the Commerce Department,[20] respectively.

The mission review process focuses primarily on the payload to be launched. Where another agency is responsible for licensing a payload, the OCST need only ascertain that such an agency has issued a license, and the mission review process for the payload ends. If no other licensing is in place, the OCST, in consultation with the Department of State and the Department of Defense will examine any national security and foreign policy interests and obligations of the United States that a proposed payload may affect. The reason for consultation with the Department of State is to ensure compliance with international agreements and identify potential foreign policy implications. The typical foreign policy consideration is the danger of interference with another nation's use of spacc. Consultations with the Department of Defense involve concerns such as the prevention of collisions between proposed payloads and classified military satellites. It is unlikely that consultations among the three agencies result in disagreements. The vagueness of the language of the act, however, could lead to potential delays and uncertainties.

As part of the information to be supplied by the applicant for the mission safety review, the OCST requires details on three major areas: launch plan, payload operation, and financial responsibility. Information on the launch plan includes a description of the launch vehicle, a flight plan, and a list of unique hazards that might be posed by either the launch or reentry. Payload operation information includes the nature and ownership of the payload. If the payload is not licensed by the FCC or the Department of Commerce, the information required will also include an assessment of safety issues, the payload's design, and the payload's proposed orbit. The required financial responsibility information includes either evidence of commercial third-party liability coverage or evidence of the purchase of a commercial surety bond. The OCST determines the amount of insurance coverage or the amount of the bond.[21]

An applicant may start the license application procedure by going through either the mission review process or the safety review process.[22] The OCST also encourages informal inquiries by applicants in order to anticipate and minimize later problems. Once a formal application is made the OCST must make a determination within 180 days. It is the OCST and not the applicant who has the duty to follow the application through the licensing process.[23]

The Launch Act does not supersede or repeal any existing federal statutes or regulations directly applicable to private launches. In practice, however, only the FCC's authority to launch communications satellites and the Department of Commerce's authority to license remote sensing satellites have been found to be directly applicable to space transportation.[24] Therefore, during the safety review process, except for those three areas, the OCST is entirely responsible for protecting the public safety. Except for what concerns the FCC and the Department of Commerce, however, the OCST may waive any existing federal statute or regulation if the waiver would be in the public interest and would not jeopardize public safety, public property, or foreign policy interests.

OTHER COUNTRIES

Other countries possess a growing public sector launch capability, but their commercial space launch industry is still relatively small. As the private sector in those countries grows, launch activities will be increasingly regulated according to national standards. There is, therefore, an increasing risk of nonuniformity.[25]

The responsibility for the use of the Space Center, and launch site, operated by the European Space Agency at Kourou in French Guyana rests with three entities:

— The Centre National d'Études Spatiales (CNES), the French space agency, is responsible for the construction and the coordination of the operations of the center.
— Arianespace is a company in charge of the sale of launch services and the management and financing for the construction of launch vehicles.
— The European Space Agency, which owns the majority of the equipment at the launch site, has responsibility for the general management of the Ariane program and the financing for construction of the facility.

In case of damage resulting from a launch accident, liability rests with these responsible entities. Unfortunately, the exact allocation of responsibility is not a simple matter because it is not governed by specific legislation but by general understandings among the three entities.[26]

Concerning the risk of damage to the property of CNES, ESA, or Arianespace, or loss of life or injury of their employees, Arianspace provides specific guarantees. In particular, an understanding is in force to the effect that, after using the launch facilities, Arianespace must return them in the same condition in which it found them. Arianespace is also required to purchase insurance coverage for an amount equal to or greater than the value of the facilities. There is also an understanding between CNES and ESA that includes a reciprocal waiver for lawsuits without the right of subrogation.[27] Concerning the liability for personal injury or property damage to third parties, the situation is very similar to that of the United States.

NOTES

1. See Peter D. Nesgos, *Commercial Space Transportation: A New Industry Emerges*, XVI Annals of Air and Space Law, 1991, p. 393.

2. B. Cheng, *United Nations Resolutions on Outer Space, "Instant International Customary Law?"* 5 Indian Journal of International Law 23, 1965, p. 37.

3. See Bruce Stockfish, *Space Transportation and the Need for a New International Legal and Institutional Regime*, XVII-II Annals of Air and Space Law, 1992, pp. 333 *et seq.*

4. *Id.*, p. 334.

5. 72 Stat. 426; 42 U.S.C.

6. 49 U.S.C. Sec. 2601–2623.

7. See Edwin Ridley Finch and Amanda Lee Moore, *Astrobusiness: A Guide to the Commerce and Law of Outer Space*, Praeger Publishers, New York, 1985, p. 62.

8. Dula, *Private Sector Activities in Outer Space*, 19 Journal of International Law. 159, 180–81 (1985), in Michael S. Straubel, *The Commercial Space Launch Act: The Regulation of Private Space Transportation*, 52 Journal of Air Law and Commerce, 1987, p. 945.

9. See Straubel, *supra*, pp. 946–947.

10. See undated publication by the Associate Director for Program Affairs, Office of Commercial Space Transportation.

11. See Straubel, *supra*, pp. 950–951.

12. The Commercial Space Launch Act, 49 U.S.C. § 2605(b)(2).

13. *Id*, at 2603(f).

14. 51 Fed. Reg. 6870, 6875 (1986) codified at 14 C.F.R. ch. 111.

15. The Chief Counsel of the FAA, in a March 11, 1977 letter, concluded that the Shuttle is not an aircraft "for purposes of the FAA respecting the applicability of the Federal Aviation Regulations (FARs)." Straubel, *supra*, p. 952.

16. See 49 U.S.C. app. 2603(11) (Supp. II, 1984).

17. See Nesgos, *supra*, p. 399.

18. 14 C.F.R 415.11.

19. 14 C.F.R. par. 415.13, in Straubel, *supra*, p. 957.

20. See 49 U.S.C. par. 2605(b)(1).

21. 49 U.S.C. par. 2614(c).

22. See 14 C.F.R. par. 411.3 (a).

23. *Id.*, 413.9.

24. See 49 U.S.C. par. 2605(c)(2).

25. See Stockfish, *supra*, p. 331.

26. See Stephane Lessard and Frederic Nordlund, *Le Base de Lancement; Évolution et Aspects Juridiques*, XV Annals of Air and Space Law, XV 1990, p. 387.

27. *Id.*

Chapter Eight

Launch Services

In Chapter 7 we have seen the general framework of space transportation as it relates to regulation of launch activities, such as application procedures, payload licensing, safety requirements and other regulatory issues. This chapter focuses on the launch services themselves, as a commercial activity.

In the early stages of space exploration, space programs had the main purpose of strengthening national security and enhancing national prestige. They were conducted almost exclusively by the government with little involvement by private industry. Space technology, developed at the height of the cold war, was also kept under tight control to protect national security. Gradually, however, the private sector began to perceive the economic potential of space ventures.[1] Commercial uses of space began but, in the United States, the government proved unable to effectively meet the new challenge.

Committing a substantial portion of its resources to the space shuttle, NASA phased out the use of unmanned expendable launch vehicles (ELVs).[2] Other countries, particularly in Europe, continued to develop ELV technology. In 1980 Arianespace, the European consortium, entered the launch commercial market and put an end to NASA's monopoly on Western commercial launches.

In the 1980s, the U.S. government, as part of its general policy of deregulation, began to encourage the privatization and commercialization of space transportation. The National Space Policy, officially unveiled on July 4, 1982, anticipated private sector involvement and investment in the development of launch services.[3] On May 16, 1983, the National Security Council issued a comprehensive policy for ELV commercialization designed to further encourage private involvement in the field.[4] In February

1984, the administration designated the Department of Transportation as the lead agency for the regulation of private ELV launching[5] and then created the Office of Commercial Space Transportation to oversee its responsibilities.

The *Commercial Space Launch Act*[6] had the purpose of encouraging entrepreneurial activity in launch services by providing for licensing and insurance requirements and the use of government property. It also provides for the U.S. government to enter international negotiations to encourage fair competition in launch services. The act is a good start for the development of a viable launch industry in the United States.

Section 2614 of the *Commercial Space Launch Act* requires the Office of Commercial Space Transportation to "facilitate and encourage" the private sector in acquiring excess government launch property and services.[7] The Senate report on the act explains that the role of OCST is to further a pricing policy that will encourage the commercial launch industry.[8] Section 2614 of the act establishes pricing guidelines. All sales, the act states, should guarantee a reasonable return to the federal government and provide no direct subsidies. How realistic that policy is is questionable, given that, directly or indirectly, the U.S. shuttle, the French Ariane, and the Russian commercial launches have all received government subsidies. To be competitive, the private launch industry may need access to low-cost government technology and services.[9]

The act did not originally deal with the details of the insurance requirement but the 1988 Amendments set out comprehensive regulation of launch insurance. The crucial part of the insurance provisions limits the liability of the launching entity to $500 million and requires that the launching entity obtain an equal amount of insurance for each launch, or the maximum obtainable on the world market, whichever is less. As a condition to this minimum insurance requirement, however, the government is obligated to require all of its entities and all contractors and subcontractors associated with the launch to file cross-waivers of liability for amounts in excess of the level of insurance.[10] Similar limits of liability have been used in the past to encourage the development of aviation and nuclear power. The wide use of cross-waivers of liability, however, is a phenomenon typical of the space industry and it basically requires each entity to absorb losses in excess of insurance. The rationale for cross-waivers is that, by avoiding excessive litigation and exposure to liability for other parties' damages, the industry has a better chance to develop.

The 1988 amendments to the act also added provisions meant to encourage research and development.[11] Section 10 of the 1988 amendments requires NASA to develop a program, in concert with the representatives of the launch industries, to encourage research and development of advanced launch technologies with higher performance and lower costs. Any technological advances would then be available to both government and commercial launch entities.[12] The government is also required by the act to make available the excess capacity at public launch sites through sale or lease at fair market prices, and to charge only "direct costs" for launch services.[13]

DEMAND AND SUPPLY FOR LAUNCH SERVICES

It can fairly be said that, although there is intense competition for the sale of launch services today, the market is not free of government intervention and sometimes restrictive regulation. General Dynamics, McDonnell-Douglas, Martin Marietta, and other large contractors of NASA and the Defense Department constitute the core of the American launch industry. There are also a number of smaller companies and start-up ventures. NASA and the other agencies of the U.S. government have for the most part withdrawn from the commercial launch arena.[14]

The Titan launch vehicle of Martin Marietta possesses the advantage of large payload capacity and is able to carry multiple satellites and other large-sized payloads. The Atlas launcher of General Dynamics is quite competitive in the small-payload market and capable of launching three smaller satellites into low earth orbit.[15] Smaller companies have a very different approach to launch activities than do traditional NASA contractors. They tend to have more flexibility and be more innovative by building new-concept launch vehicles, or using old technology in new ways. Smaller companies seem to be able to produce competitively priced launchers. Small-payload launchers, however, are vulnerable to launch failures because their capital is relatively small. Also, they do not have a presence in the lucrative communications satellite market.[16]

As noted earlier, due in part to the lack of government direction in the seventies and early eighties, foreign aerospace companies have aggressively entered the market for launch services, including the U.S. market. Several foreign countries have heavily invested in the aerospace field for national security reasons or to acquire a lead in technology. Taking advantage of the interruption of space launches in the United States caused by the Challenger accident, foreign launching entities have developed the capability to supply the equivalent of six to ten shuttle launches per year through the rest of the 1990s.[17]

In 1980, the European Space Agency transferred its launch services program to Arianespace, a French corporation that has now become a leader in the field and has won over half of all contracts for future launches. In order to further strengthen its position and to achieve the economy of scale that American launchers achieve thanks to government procurement, the company has concluded four general agreements with European subcontractors for the production of 50 additional Ariane 4 launchers over the next few years.[18] The dominance of Arianspace has made it difficult for private companies in Europe to enter the launch market.

Initially, Japan was using a launch technology developed from the American Delta, but that technology was transferred on the condition that it not be used for commercial launches. Japan is now developing its own rocket using local technology. The ability of Japan to enter the commercial launch market is also hindered by the fact that its launch facility can only be used for part of the year.[19] The Chinese have also become involved in the commercial launch business with their Long March 3 and Long March 4 rockets. Because of the low pricing of these launches there has been a certain measure of trade controversy, which is highlighted by export licensing requirements for American satellites.

The former Soviet Union, which for the purposes of commercial space is mainly the Russian Federation and Kazakhstan, has a long tradition of launch activities that it is now offering on a commercial basis to many users around the world. The Russians have a broad range of launch vehicles and, for certain types of space transportation, their only competitor is NASA. Several developing countries are also starting to become involved in launch activities but their immediate goal is not so much to enter the commercial market but to avoid being dependent on the space powers.

The demand for launch services has not kept pace with the supply in recent years so that a glut has resulted and will probably continue through most of the nineties. About 75 percent of such demand comes from the public sector, such as space agencies, weather services, defense departments, research institutions under government control, and others.[20] Only part of these customers, however, will make use of private launch services. In spite of the better economic terms generally offered by private companies, political and noneconomic concerns tend to dictate the use of government services. Private launchers must therefore essentially rely on commercial demand for most of their business. Although the commercial space sector is very promising for the future, at present, only the communications satellite business is profitable enough to pay for itself. Other markets such as remote sensing, materials processing, and scientific exploration may offer prospects of economic benefits but still require substantial government participation.

LAUNCH SERVICES AGREEMENTS

Looking more closely at the specific launch service activity, from a legal standpoint it is essential to understand the issues and concerns presented by the interaction between launcher entities and their customers. Launch service agreements are conceptually no different from other contracts involving high-tech ventures, but there are some provisions that are unique to the field.

Launch service agreements incorporate clauses that have become customary over the years in both the launch service and the satellite purchase areas.

As is the case in most contracts, and particularly in satellite purchase agreements, the scope of work must clearly be defined. In this type of contract what is being purchased is not hardware but a service, that is, the service of integrating and launching the spacecraft into orbit. This involves not only the launch itself, but also prelaunch preparation, payload processing and integration of the payload with the launch vehicle. In general, the launch entity will be responsible up until the launch ignition commences except for the delivery of postlaunch telemetry data.[21]

The launch schedule is another important provision, and it should spell out launch postponement rights that the parties may have. Usually, the customer, that is, the owner or operator of the satellite to be launched, does not earn revenues until the satellite is in orbit. Further, the business plan may anticipate a launch within a certain period of time and commitments may already have been made to satellite users. From the perspective of the launch company, however, flexibility is important to deal with possible technical anomalies or government priorities.[22]

The next provision to be included in a launch service agreement is a schedule of payments. As noted earlier, the customer in a launch service does not normally earn revenues until the satellite is in orbit and operational. The launch company, on the other hand, faces expenses from the prelaunch activity all the way up to ignition. A payments schedule chart is therefore the result of careful negotiation for which there is no standard format.

As in satellite purchase agreements, it is essential to include a provision on the allocation of risks. Launch activities are expensive ventures and notoriously risky. Not only do parties have responsibilities among themselves, but also toward other participants in the launch activities as well as third parties who are not involved. The risks are indeed many. The first obvious possibility is that of a complete launch failure or of shutdown of the engines immediately after ignition. The launch could also be a complete or partial failure if it places the satellite in the wrong orbit. The second is that of property damage, which in most cases is the loss of the spacecraft or other related equipment. Third-party liability is also a serious issue that is usually dealt with by the parties getting insurance as appropriate. For the launch activity itself there are several stage-types of insurance available, including prelaunch insurance, ground property insurance for abort, launch, and initial operations insurance/launch risk guarantee.[23]

A provision is also necessary related to permits, such as export licenses and other government authorizations. As we saw in Chapter 7, the *Commercial Space Launch Act* governs commercial launch activities and the Office of Commercial Space Transportation is in charge of licensing launch companies. The launch company will therefore be responsible for obtaining all the necessary permits relating to the launch itself. It will usually also assist with the import permits and authorization that may be required for a satellite. Also, because the customer ordinarily obtains no intellectual property rights in connection with the launch services, the launch company should take responsibility for any patent or intellectual property infringement.[24]

As in other contracts, a choice of law provision as well as an arbitration clause are customary in order to achieve a timely resolution of disputes. The rules of the American Arbitration Association or the International Chamber of Commerce are often incorporated in the agreement.

NOTES

1. See Timothy A. Brooks, *Regulating International Trade in Launch Services*, 6 High Technology Law Journal, 1991, pp. 59–107.
2. *See* Logdson, *The Space Shuttle Program: A Policy Failure?*, 232 Science, 1986, pp. 1099, 1100–1101.
3. Robinson and Meredith, *Domestic Commercialization of Space: The Current Political Atmosphere*, 1 American Enterprise, The Law, and the Commercial Use of Space, 1986.
4. Dula, *Private Sector Activities in Outer Space*, 19 International Law, 1986, pp. 159, 183.
5. Executive Order 12465 of February 24, 1984.
6. Pub. Law No. 98–575, 98 Stat. 3055, amended by Commercial Space Launch Act Amendments of 1988, Pub. Law No. 100–657, 102 Stat. 3900 (codified as amended at 49 U.S.C. §§ 2601–2623 [1988]).
7. Michael S. Straubel, *The Commercial Space Launch Act: The Regulation of Private Space Transportation*, 52 Journal of Air Law and Commerce, 1987, pp. 964–965.
8. Senate Report 656, reprinted in 1984 U.S. Code Cong. & Admin. News, at 5342.

9. See Straubel, *supra*, at 965.

10. 49 U.S.C. § 2615(a)(1) (A) and (D)(1988).

11. See Brooks, *supra*, at 62.

12. Commercial Space Launch Act Amendments of 1988, Pub. Law No. 100–657, § 10, 102 Stat. 3900, 3907 (1988).

13. 49 U.S.C. § 2514 (a), (b) (b)(1) (1988).

14. See Brooks, *supra*, at 64–65.

15. *Single Atlas to Launch Three Small Satellites*, Aviation Week and Space Technology, March 26, 1990, p. 24.

16. See Brooks, *supra*, at 67.

17. *Setting Space Transportation Policy for the 1990's*, Congressional Budget Office, 1986, p. 23.

18. *Arianespace Racks up Launch Business: Ariane 5 Set for Launch in 1995*, Aviation Week and Space Technology, November 27, 1989 at S. 4., quoted in Brooks, *supra*, at 69.

19. Swinkbanks, *First Setback for Japan*, 340 Nature, 1989, p. 493.

20. Brooks, *supra*, at 74.

21. Peter D. Nesgos, *Legal Aspects of Space Commercialization. Contracts and Insurance Issues in Telecommunications Satellite Projects*, remarks at International Space University, 1992 Summer Session, Kitakyushu, Japan, August 11, 1992, at p. 7 of edited transcripts.

22. *Id.*

23. *Ibid*, Risk Timeline table.

24. *Id*, at pp. 9–10.

Chapter Nine

Antitrust and Trade Issues

The magnitude of investments and sophisticated know-how required for space ventures tends to favor the development of a market dominated by large companies. Although the policy of encouraging competition is a sound one, in the space field there are at least two reasons for mitigating some of the effects of the antitrust laws. The first one is that, aside from the distortions created by government participation, some of the space endeavors require a long time to accomplish, with uncertainty as to the economic benefits accruing to the companies involved. They usually also require enormous capital and access to cutting edge technology and proprietary data. It would therefore be unrealistic to expect the emergence of a large number of small- to medium-sized companies in a perfectly balanced and competitive market. Some of the largest projects are indeed best undertaken in the form of joint ventures or cooperation between large entities. The other factor to be considered is that, even if the United States were to enact and enforce very strict antitrust laws, there is no guarantee that other countries would do the same. Because aerospace activities are for the most part transnational or multinational, U.S. companies would operate at a disadvantage if they were artificially broken down and had to compete with huge foreign entities and foreign governments. Following is a brief description of the U.S. and foreign antitrust laws as they apply to aerospace activities.

The antitrust laws of the European Union are contained in Article 85 of the *Treaty of Rome*,[1] which provides in part that:

> the following shall be prohibited as incompatible with the common market: all agreements between undertakings, decisions by associations of undertakings and concerted practices which may affect trade between Member States and which have

as their object or effect the prevention, restriction or distortion of competition within the common market, and in particular those that:

a. directly or indirectly fix purchase or selling prices or any other trading conditions;
b. limit or control production, markets, technical development, or investment;
c. share markets or sources of supply;
d. apply dissimilar conditions to equivalent transactions with other trading parties, thereby placing them at a competitive disadvantage;
e. make the conclusion of contracts subject to the acceptance by other parties of supplementary obligations which, by their nature or according to commercial usage, have no connection with the subject of such contracts."

Section 3 of Article 85, however, gives parties the right to request exemptions from the European Community Commission. In particular, the section provides that

the provision of Article 85(1) may be declared inapplicable in the case of:

— any agreement or category of agreements between undertakings
— any decision or category of decisions
— any concerted practice or category of concerted practices; which contributes to improving the production or distribution of goods or to promote the technical or economic progress, while allowing consumers a fair share of the resulting benefit, and which does not:
  a. impose on the undertaking concerned restrictions which are not indispensable to the attainment of these objectives;
  b. afford such undertakings the possibility of eliminating competition in respect of a substantial part of the products in question.

Because the commission holds the exclusive right to grant exemptions under Article 85, it controls antitrust enforcement in the EU.[2] In 1984, the commission adopted a Commission Regulation that gives automatic exemption for three types of research and development joint ventures: (1) joint R&D coupled with joint exploitation results; (2) joint exploitation of prior R&D results; and (3) joint R&D without joint exploitation of results for agreements falling within the scope of Article 85(1).[3] Although joint exploitation does not include sale or distribution, it does include manufacturing and licensing. In the case of pharmaceuticals developed in space, for example, companies from the EU can engage in both R&D joint ventures and production joint ventures insulated from antitrust liability. The commission is also considering additional exceptions to its competition rules.[4]

The antitrust laws of Japan are notoriously ineffective when compared to American or even European legislation. The basic antitrust law is the *Act*

Concerning the Prohibition of Private Monopoly and Maintenance of Fair Trade (*Anti-Monopoly Act*).[5] That act was modeled on American competitive laws, but since then the policy in Japan has been to encourage R&D and production joint ventures through government financial support, tax incentives, and relaxation of antitrust laws. Enforcement of the act is the responsibility of the Japanese Fair Trade Commission (JFTC), which exercises quasi-judicial and quasi-legislative power.[6] The reason for the ineffectiveness of the antitrust system in Japan is that, although the JFTC has the power to bring both civil and criminal actions, civil penalties are negligible and criminal actions are almost never brought. Under the act, there is a private right of action, but plaintiffs are rare and none seem to prevail in the Japanese courts.[7]

The antitrust laws of the United States are, by far, the strictest in the world and place American firms at a disadvantage with foreign competitors who face less restrictions on joint ventures and other similar type of arrangements.

Section 1 of the *Sherman Act*[8] states that: "Every contract, combination in the form of trust or otherwise, or conspiracy, in restraint of trade or commerce among the several states, or with foreign nations, is declared illegal."

In addition, U.S. law also contains restrictions affecting mergers and acquisitions of companies. Section 18 of the *Clayton Act*[9] provides that

> No person engaged in commerce or any activity affecting commerce shall acquire, directly or indirectly, the whole or any part of the stock or other share capital and no person subject to the jurisdiction of the Federal Trade Commission shall acquire the whole or any part of the assets of another person engaged also in commerce or in any activity effecting commerce, where in any line of commerce or in any activity effecting commerce in any section of the country, the effect of such acquisition may be to substantially lessen competition, or to tend to create a monopoly.

These laws contain treble damages provisions that encourage parties to sue. Courts also tend to interpret the antitrust laws in a broad way. The result of this strict enforcement, as was noted earlier, has been to place American firms at a competitive disadvantage in the global market. In order to mitigate this problem, the *National Cooperative Research Act* (NCRA) was enacted in 1984.[10] The basic purpose of the act is to limit damages that plaintiffs in an antitrust lawsuit can recover to actual damages in the area of joint research activities. Such activities are defined by the act as follows:

> The term "joint research and development venture" means any group of activities, including attempting to make, making, or performing a contract by two or more persons for the purpose of-

a. theoretical analysis, experimentation, or systematic study of phenomena or observable facts,
b. the development or testing of basic engineering techniques,
c. the extension of investigative findings or theory of a scientific or technical nature into practical application for experimental or demonstration purposes, including the experimental production and testing of models, prototypes, equipment, materials and processes,
d. the collection, exchange, and analysis of research information, or
e. any combination of the purposes specified in subparagraphs (A), (B) and (D), and may include the establishment and operation of facilities for the conducting of research, the conducting of such venture on a protected and proprietary basis, and the prosecuting of applications for patents and the granting of licenses for the results of such venture, but does not include any activity specified in subsection (b).[11]

The NCRA also limits the scope of Section 1 of the *Sherman Act* by codifying the so-called "rule of reason," which had been left to the courts to interpret. Section 4302 of the NCRA provides that:

In any action under the antitrust laws, or under any State law similar to the antitrust laws, the conduct of any person in making or performing a contract to carry out a joint research and development venture shall not be deemed illegal per se; such conduct will be judged on the basis of its reasonableness, taking into account all relevant factors affecting competition, including, but not limited to, effects on competition in properly defined, relevant research and development markets.

American companies involved in the aerospace business, in addition to the antitrust laws, however mitigated by the NCRA and other proposed legislation, also have to deal with dumping, and other unfair trade practices of competitors from several countries. That is true particularly in the field of launch services where the United States government has made several attempts to assist domestic companies.

Section 303 of the *Tariff Act of 1930*[12] provides that if the U.S. International Trade Commission (ITC) finds that any country "shall pay or bestow, directly or indirectly, any bounty or grant upon the manufacture or production or export, of any article of merchandise manufactured or produced in such a country" it must apply a countervailing duty equal to the "net amount of such bounty or grant." Section 701 of the *Subsidies Code*[13] of the *General Agreement on Tariffs and Trade* (GATT), however, supersedes Section 303 of the *Tariff Act of 1930.* Section 701 adds an injury requirement to the basic rule of Section 303 and replaces the term "bounty or grant" with "subsidy."[14] Subsidies are countervailable if they are aimed primarily at the export market, or if they are "domestic" subsidies that provide a specific benefit to the producer.[15] Specific benefits are those provided to the producer alone rather than the general public. The measure of the subsidy is considered to be the cost advantage of the government-provided services over their price in the open market.[16]

Unfairly priced imports are also dealt with by antidumping laws. Section 731 of the *Tariff Act* targets goods priced at "less than fair value."[17] Antidumping investigations may be initiated by the International Trade Administration (ITA) or, as in countervailing duty investigations, by private petitions through the ITC.[18]

Services traditionally have not been covered by international and domestic antidumping regulations. Section 731 only applies to "merchandise," which parallels the GATT antidumping coverage, also limited to "products" and the corresponding provision of the *Antidumping Act of 1916*, which refers to "articles" imported into the United States.[19] There are efforts being made, however, at both the national and international level to expand the antidumping regulations to services.

In addition to the already mentioned antidumping laws and countervailing duties, unfair trade practices are addressed by Section 301 of the *Trade Act of 1974*,[20] and Section 337 of the *Tariff Act of 1930*.[21] Section 301 gives the United States Trade Representative (USTR) extensive power to counter unfair trade practices by foreign governments and also provides remedies for unfair trade in services. It is not limited to imports, but applies to any unjust injury to U.S. commerce.[22] The definition of what constitutes unfair trade practices under Section 301 is quite broad and allows the USTR to impose sanctions against countries that have unfairly restricted U.S. trade or denied U.S. rights under any trade agreement.[23] The strongest and most glamorous provisions in the Act are the "Super 301" which grant the USTR the right to act on a long list of violations, including barriers to entry, government tolerance of antitrust violations, export targeting, unfair labor practices, inadequate intellectual property protection, and closed service sectors.[24]

Under Section 301, the USTR may initiate an action on its own or start an investigation on the petition of a private party. The latter procedure is the preferred one because it gives the government a more neutral stance. Several firms in the space services industry have availed themselves of Section 301 to redress unfair trade practices. Several attempts have met with success with regard to Japan, which is moving in the direction of opening government procurement of satellites to foreign companies.[25]

Relief against unfair trade practices is also provided by Section 337 of the *Tariff Act of 1930*. In response to a private petition, the act requires the International Trade Commission to conduct investigations of unfair trade practices other than those requiring antidumping penalties or countervailing duties and to exclude the importation of offending items.[26]

NOTES

1. Treaty Establishing the European Economic Community, March 25, 1957, art. 85, 298 U.N.T.S. 11, 47.

2. John F. Kohler, *Space Pharmaceuticals: Will the United States Fumble Another High Technology Industry?* 58 Journal of Air Law and Commerce #2, Winter 1992, pp. 518–520.

3. Commission Regulation (EEC) 418/85 of December 19, 1984, on the Application of Article 85(3) of the Treaty to Categories of Research and Development Agreements, 1985 O. J. Eur. Comm. Legislation (153) 5 (February 22, 1985).

4. See Kohler, *supra.*

5. Shiteki dokusen no kinshi oyobi Kosei Torihiki no Kakuho ni kansuru Horitsu, Act No. 516, 1947, translated in Hiroshi Iyori and Akinori Uesugi, *The Antimonopoly Laws of Japan* 213–64 (1983), in Kohler, *supra*, p. 517.

6. Preston Moore, *Antitrust Aspects of Technology Exploitation in Japan*, in International Antitrust 32.031, 32.035, William A Hancock ed., 1991.

7. See Kohler, *supra*, at 518.

8. 15 U.S.C. § 1 (1988).

9. 5 U.S.C. § 18 (1988).

10. 15 U.S.C. §§ 4301–4305.

11. 15 U.S.C. § 4301 (6).

12. 19 U.S.C. § 1303 (1988).

13. Agreement on Interpretation and Application of Articles VI, XVI, and XXIII of the General Agreement on Tariffs and Trade, opened for signature June 30, 1979, GATT Basic Instruments and Selected Documents 58–83 (26th Supp. 1980) [hereinafter Subsidies Code).

14. 19 U.S.C. § 1671 (1988).

15. 19 U.S.C. § 1677 (A) (ii) (1988). Also see Timothy A. Brooks, *Regulating International Trade Launch Services*, 6 High Technology Law Journal, 1991, p. 88.

16. See Brooks, *ibid.*

17. 19 U.S.C. § 1673 (1).

18. *Id.*, § 1673 a(a) and a(b).

19. See Brooks, *supra*, at 89.

20. 19 U.S.C. § 2411 (1988).

21. *Id.*, § 1337.

22. *Id.*, § 2411 (c)(1)(B) and (B)(ii).

23. *Id.*, § 2411(a)(1)(A) and (a)(1)(B)(ii).

24. See Brooks, *supra*, at 92.

25. *Id.*

26. 19 U.S.C. § 1337(b)(1); (b)(3); § 1337(d), in Brooks, *supra*, at 94.

Chapter Ten

Intellectual Property

As commercial aerospace activities increase over the years, it is becoming ever more important to resolve issues such as the protection of data, products, and ideas to safeguard the potential of the industry. Private firms investing in commercial space ventures spend large amounts of money over extended periods of time before a return on their investment can be expected. Those firms will require assurance that they can protect the inventions and products resulting from their space activities as a condition to risking large amounts of capital.[1] The categories of intellectual property can be generally classified as trade secrets, proprietary data, industrial property rights, copyrights, trademarks, and patents.

GENERAL CONCEPTS

At the core of intellectual property protection is the concept of trade secret. In the United States, trade secret law is created by common law and trade statute rather than through federal laws. Trade secret law may therefore vary from state to state. The general concepts, however, are reasonably uniform. It can be said generally that trade secret encompasses any information that is not generally known and gives one competitor an advantage over another. Trade secret principles are broader than those of patent or copyright and can include ideas as well as inventions and particular works of authorship. The protection of trade secrets is relatively inexpensive to maintain through a process of security measures, secrecy agreements, and properly drafted licenses. Trade secret status, however, unlike patents, provides no protection against independent development of similar ideas, processes, or formulas. From an international point of view, there are also countries that do not have a general "trade secret" law and the only protection is left to contractual agreements between parties.[2]

Copyright is designed to protect original works of authorship fixed in a tangible medium of expression. In the United States, the subject is covered by federal statutes. Copyright protection, however, is limited by the fact that only the form or manner of expression is protected and not the concepts or ideas embodied in the authored work. Until March 1, 1989, a copyright in the United States was lost if it was published without the statutorily required notice, which consists of the word "copyright," or the copy symbol, with the name of the copyright owner and the date of publication. The notice is no longer required but it is still desirable in proving infringement damages. A copyright can be registered with the Copyright Office of the Library of Congress. Registration is not required to create the copyright, but U.S. citizens should register it before a federal court will enforce the copyright. Registration also has an effect on the availability of statutorily provided damages. A company involved in commercial space activities should therefore mark with a copyright notice published materials created for it by an employee and should also consider its copyrights on important works.[3] Industrial property, also known as know-how, includes patents and utility models, plant variety rights, industrial designs, and other similar concepts.

TRADEMARKS

Another category of intellectual property is the trademark, which consists of those names and symbols under which a company conducts business. It is a sign that serves to distinguish the product of one company from the products of others. As the goodwill of a successful company tends to increase in value with the passage of time, a company should take care, early in its existence, to adopt marks that are capable of being protected as trademarks and protect them. To be registered as a trademark a sign must be visible rather than audible. Visible signs that may be registered include invented words, names, letters, symbols, and pictures. Very similar to trademarks are trade names, appellations of origin, and indications of source. Registration of a trademark in the United States is done at the U.S. Patent and Trademark Office.

As with patents and designs, most countries have enacted statutes for the registration and protection of that type of property right. Among the international trade mark agreements are the following.

Madrid Agreement Concerning the International Registration of Marks. The agreement, which came into force on July 15, 1892, provides a simplified procedure for entities or persons wishing to secure trademark protection in a number of countries. Where a person has obtained registration of a trademark in a country that is a signatory to the Madrid Agreement, that person may, by filing a single application with the International Bureau of the World Intellectual Property Organization (WIPO), obtain protection for 20 years in any other signatory countries that the applicant may choose.

Trademark Registration Treaty (TRT). The treaty, which was adopted by the Vienna diplomatic conference on June 12, 1973, came into effect on August 7, 1980. Under the TRT, a trademark need not be registered at the national level. A single application is filed by the owner with the International Bureau of WIPO and is valid into all signatory states.

The Nice Agreement Concerning the International Classification of Goods and Services for the Purposes of the Registration of Marks establishes a list of 42 classes of goods and services. It entered into force on April 8, 1961, and was revised in Stockholm in 1967 and Geneva in 1977. It has been widely adopted.

The *Vienna Agreement Establishing an International Classification of the Figurative Elements of Marks* deals with device marks and classifies all trademarks comprising emblems, symbols, or pictures. It entered into force on August 9, 1985.

The Lisbon Agreement for the Protection of Appellations of Origin came into force in 1958 and provides for the protection of only those geographic locations that attribute a physical quality to the goods.[4]

PATENTS

Unlike trade secret protection, patent protection requires the disclosure of the subject matter to be patented. Patents can be granted for processes, machines, and any new and useful improvement of processes, technology, and the like. A grant of patent rights provides a 17-year monopoly period during which even those who might independently arrive at the same invention would be prohibited from using it commercially. Issuance of a patent, however, means that the trade secrets incorporated in it are no longer trade secrets. If the basic value of an invention consists of an idea, concept, or know-how or other unpatentable aspects of the invention, patent protection is unsuitable. Obtaining a patent is also expensive and could involve an extended period of time.[5]

In only a few years, we have seen a remarkable transformation of technology-intensive industries. Private enterprise has, quite literally, launched itself into space with a degree of inventiveness and enthusiasm that brings back memories of the early days of the Mercury Seven astronauts and the Apollo moon program. These corporate explorers have discovered that space, an environment where things happen differently than on earth, offers unique opportunities for new discoveries.[6] Space, with its absence of vibration, sterile environment, unfiltered sunlight, near-perfect vacuum, and microgravity, provides a perfect condition for the production of certain chemicals and pharmaceuticals. Because earth's gravity concentrates sediment and other impurities during the production of drugs, thereby reducing purity and yield, many companies would prefer to produce some of their pharmaceuticals in space.[7] In fact, experiments are already being conducted in space including one where McDonnell Douglas produced a drug 716 times more separated than could be produced on earth with five times greater purity.[8] Among the many challenges that the pharmaceutical industry faces in this new exciting frontier is the safeguarding of its inventions and products, which, as we have seen, would require patent protection, one of the most complex legal issues under both traditional and space law.

As we have seen, the bulk of the so-called space law consists of the United Nations treaties, namely the *Treaty on Principles Governing the Activities of States in the Exploration and Use of Outer Space, Including the Moon and Other Celestial Bodies*, commonly referred to as the Outer Space Treaty[9] and the other agreements (the *Astronauts Rescue Agreement,*[10] the Liability Convention[11], the *Registration Convention*[12] and the *Moon Treaty*[13]). Although those treaties primarily address space activities of sovereign states, they also take into account activities of private entities. The existing law of outer space lays several significant obligations and restrictions on private ventures in space. For example, Article I of the 1967 Outer Space Treaty provides that private space activities are to be for peaceful purposes and carried out for the benefit of all countries. According to Article VI of the treaty, private space activities must also be under the authorization and continuing supervision of the launching state, with that state bearing international responsibility for them.

Although international space law does not deal with the protection of private interests and intellectual property rights, a highly debated issue is the meaning of "space activities carried out for the benefit and interests of all countries" of Article I of the Outer Space Treaty. In the United States, that phrase has mostly been interpreted to mean that all countries should share in the benefits of space activities, but not that any country must share its proprietary technology or its profits.[14] The Moon Treaty may raise the question (so far only theoretical) of whether the concept of "common heritage of mankind" embodied in that treaty would extend to proprietary technology. The United States has not ratified the Moon Treaty nor does it accept the meaning of "common heritage" as common ownership of space resources and majority control over their disposition.[15] As has been explained, it would be unreasonable to expect that private capital flow to activities without the prospect of a return on the investment.

Aside from space law proper, there are several international treaties relating to patents that should be kept in mind. They are the following.

Paris Convention for the Protection of Industrial Property. Originally adopted in 1883, the convention has undergone a number of significant revisions. It basically deals with four topics: (1) substantive rules of law guaranteeing the right of national treatment; (2) rules that guarantee the right of priority (3) rules relating to specific topics of industrial property law, and (4) the establishment of an administrative framework for the implementation of the convention. The national treatment principle provides that parties to the convention must grant the same industrial property protection to nationals of other member states as it grants to its own nationals. The right of priority, under Article 4, means that on the basis of an application for an industrial property right filed by an applicant in a member country, the same applicant may apply for protection in all other member states. In the patents context, the priority principle means that an applicant for registration in a member country will be protected from the loss of novelty by any exploitation of the patent during the priority period in any other member country.

Patent Cooperation Treaty. The treaty was established by a Washington conference in 1970 with the goal of rendering more affordable the international protection for patents. The treaty provides for the filing of a single application for patent registration. The filing is effective in all countries designated in the application that are parties to the treaty. The application is subject to an international search by a designated searching authority. The application and search report are then transmitted by WIPO to all relevant patent offices. A very practical benefit of the treaty is the establishment of a facility for a preliminary international search of an invention's novelty and industrial applicability to assess whether it is worth the expense of the application.[16]

Strasbourg Convention on the International Classification of Patents of 1971. Patents are classified according to the technical field to which they relate and are given a serial number within a patent office. In order to provide a common basis for the search of patent documents, the convention established the International Patent Classification (IPC), which is administered by WIPO.[17]

U.S. and international patent law present many complex issues. The United States is one of two or three countries in the world to utilize the first-to-invent patent system, under which patents are granted to the first party to prove invention of a particular item. The patent systems used in both Europe and Japan, on the other hand, are first-to-file systems with no regard to who actually made the invention first. This difference may have serious consequences for pharmaceutical companies trying to protect new products developed in space. U.S. pharmaceutical companies usually have to choose between statutory patent protection or common law trade secret protection. By choosing to file for patent protection under the U.S. first-to-invent system they may limit their effective protection to the U.S. market because they are vulnerable to European and Japanese companies who may win the race in their first-to-file system. This danger holds U.S. firms back from R&D because the risk may just be too high even though U.S. companies may be able to file first even for inventions of others and thereby gain the patent.[18]

There are several other problems specifically related to the patenting of medical technology that adversely affect U.S. pharmaceutical companies. To obtain a U.S. patent, the applicant must file a patent application describing at least one embodiment of the invention in sufficient detail to enable any person skilled in the field to make and use the invention.[19] Because medical inventions are by their nature different from mechanical inventions, different types of patent practices have evolved that offer little protection to holders of medical patents or deny the patent altogether. In addition, lengthy Food and Drug Administration (FDA) investigatory and premarket clearance procedures tend to reduce the useful life of medical patents.[20] There is also the problem that many developing countries refuse to give protection to such patents on the ground that they consider their right to copy the inventions as vital to their national well being.

In addition to the mentioned obstacles in protecting inventions, until November 1990, U.S. pharmaceutical companies also faced the problem that U.S. patent law had an exclusively terrestrial application, limiting the protection it provided to the United States, its territories, and possessions.[21] Even the U.S. Supreme Court, in 1972, emphasized that U.S. patent law had no extraterritorial effect.[22] The *Patents Law Amendments Act*[23] of 1984 did little to alleviate the concern of the industry.

An important step in addressing the problem of extraterritoriality came with the *Space Patent Act of 1990*,[24] which accomplished two major goals, best expressed by the following Report of Congress:[25]

> Section 105(a) provides that any invention made, used or sold on a space object in outer space shall be considered to have been made, used or sold within the United States in two cases.
>
> The first case hinges on U.S. jurisdiction or control. Specifically, activities occurring on space objects under the "jurisdiction or control of the United States"

are considered to have occurred in the United States, unless one of the two following exceptions apply.

First, an invention made, used or sold on a space object or component thereof under the jurisdiction or control of the United States while in outer space will not be considered to have been made, used or sold in the United States if such object or component thereof is specifically identified and otherwise provided for in an international agreement to which the United States is a party. Such exception may be for one or more of the purposes of title 35 (of the U.S. Code) relating to either the making, using, or selling of an invention in the United States as applicable.

The flexibility provided by this exception is considered important in negotiating international agreements relating to cooperative activities in outer space. It is particularly desirable with respect to various national laws requiring the review of filed patent applications for national security and related purposes.

The second exception provides that an invention made, used or sold on a space object or component thereof under the jurisdiction or control of the United States while in outer space will not be considered to have been made, used or sold in the United States, if such object or component is registered by a foreign state in accordance with the Convention on Registration of Objects Launched into Outer Space.

Section (105 b) provides a second basis for considering the invention-related activities of section 105 to have occurred in the United States. Unlike section (105 a), section (105 b) is not dependent on U.S. jurisdiction or control. Rather, inventions used, made or sold on any space object or component thereof, irrespective of U.S. jurisdiction or control, may be considered to have been made, used or sold in the United States where an international agreement between the United States and the State of registry specifically so provides.

This additional exception is intended to offer a domestic legal basis for implementing agreements with a foreign state of registry that provide for the application of section 105 to space objects registered by that state. This second exception is the converse or complement to the first exception for those space objects that are under the jurisdiction or control of the United States but are otherwise provided for in an international agreement.

Normally, the passage of the *Space Patent Act*, which extends U.S. patent laws to outer space, would make the question of whether the Space Treaty mandates prepatent disclosure of patentable inventions a moot issue, because the most recent patent law would replace any requirement existing in the older law. The *Space Patent Act*, however, leaves open the possibility that it does not always apply to space objects when they are "otherwise provided for by an international agreement of which the United States is a party."[26] Therefore, it is not clear whether Congress intended the *Space Patent Act* to abrogate the prepatent disclosure provisions that can be read into the Space Treaty.

In light of the outlined issues, it is important to determine whether the Space Treaty actually ever became effective U.S. law. A signed and ratified treaty, such as the Space Treaty, normally becomes the supreme law of the land if it is self-executing. If a treaty is too vague or broadly worded to stand alone, however, it would then require implementing legislation.[27] The extent to which an international agreement establishes affirmative and judicially enforceable obligations without implementing legislation must be determined in each case by reference to many contextual factors such as the purposes of the treaty and the objectives of its creators, the existence of domestic procedures and institutions appropriate for direct implementation, the availability and feasibility of alternative enforcement methods, and the immediate and long-range social consequences of self- or non-self-execution.[28]

The question of disclosure requirements that can be read into the Space Treaty can probably be answered to the effect that Congress intended to abrogate them with the *Space Patent Act.* The act was passed specifically to apply U.S. patent law to U.S.-flagged spacecraft. Congress borrowed the term "space object" from the Space Treaty for use in the statute and intended the term to have the broadest possible meaning. This section of the patent laws represents a deliberate departure from previous practice, indicating that Congress meant the term to encompass national jurisdiction as used in the Space Treaty rather than the territorial jurisdiction intended for U.S. patent law by the Supreme Court. The intent of Congress was clearly to protect U.S. concerns conducting research in space under U.S. patent laws and to abrogate any disclosure requirements that the Space Treaty could impose to the detriment of U.S. research and development in space.[29] The intent of Congress to fully protect U.S. patent holders from any form of international disclosure is brought home by a statement of the chairman of a Hearing on the Patents and Space Act[30] who stated that the four principal objectives of the bill were (1) providing that actions occurring in outer space can infringe on U.S. patent law, (2) assuring that the United States' "first to invent system" was extended to space inventions, (3) regulating "prior art," and (4) protecting security by insuring that space inventions are covered by the *Invention Security Act.*

Patent protection is obviously not only a concern of the United States but of other countries as well. As European activity in space has evolved, so have its laws with respect to intellectual property. On the scientific side, the European Space Research Organisation (ESRO) in Article III of its charter states that "the scientific results of experiments carried out with the assistance of the Organization shall be published or otherwise made generally available. After prior use by the scientists responsible for the experiments, the reduced data resulting from such experiments shall be the property of the Organization."[31] Paragraph 2 of the article provided that ESRO would publish such technical results "subject to patent rights."[32] By 1967, the ESRO Council had established a standard practice to keep intellectual property rights with contractors.

The European Launcher Development Organisation (ELDO), in Article 8 of its Convention,[33] provided that all technical information made available to ELDO, including that which covered "patents or other forms of legal protection" could be used by ELDO "for the carrying out of its programmes without payment."[34] Member states of the organization were also authorized to "use such information for any purposes of their own without payment" and could make it available to individuals and entities under their jurisdiction, subject to use within the field of space technology and contractual limitations to retain the information within the territories of the member states.[35]

Article III of the European Space Agency Convention provides that

> when placing contracts or entering into agreements, the Agency shall, with regard to the resulting inventions and technical data, secure such rights as may be appropriate for the protection of its interests, of those of the Member States participating in the relevant program, and of those of persons and bodies under their jurisdiction. These rights shall include in particular the rights of access, of disclosure, and of use. Such inventions and technical data shall be communicated to the participating States.[36]

Both ESA and ELDO have a system that results in the organization and participating states having royalty-free licensing rights for space applications in Europe. The reason for this free transfer of intellectual property is probably intended to stimulate European industrial cooperation in high-technology areas related to space, and thereby to improve the overall competitiveness of European industry.[37]

COPYRIGHT

The protection of copyrighted material, as technology for satellite transmission has progressed, has become an important priority. Protecting copyrighted works transmitted by satellite from unauthorized interception and use has been a challenge for the international community for three decades. International communications law, as embodied in the *International Telecommunication Convention* and the *Radio Regulations* of the International Telecommunications Union (ITU) is inadequate to provide sufficient protection for copyrighted material transmitted by satellite.[38] Article 22 of the Convention and Article 17 of the regulations provide that member states must keep certain telecommunications secret but their application to the interception of satellite signals is not clear. ITU sanctions are probably not strong enough to make these statutes a serious enforcing mechanism. To be sure, there are international treaties which deal with the protection of copyright but they do not address the problem of unauthorized reception of satellite transmissions. Those treaties are the *Universal Copyright Convention* (UCC) and the *Berne Convention for the Protection of Literary and Artistic Works*.[39] Aware of this gap in legislation on copyright protection, several United Nations organs began working on legislation to address the problem. In May 1974, the World Intellectual Property Organization and the United Nations Educational Scientific and Cultural Organization (UNESCO) convened in Brussels a diplomatic conference to draft a new international agreement. From that conference resulted the *Convention Relating to the Distribution of Program-Carrying Signals Transmitted by Satellite*, commonly known as the Brussels Satellite Convention, which was opened for signature on May 21, 1974, entered into force on August 25, 1979, and ratified by the United States on December 7, 1984.

Parties to the convention pledge to take "adequate measures to prevent the distribution on or from its territory of any program-carrying signal by a distributor for whom the signal emitted to or passing through the satellite is not intended." The convention, however, deals with transmission signals and not with the messages that those signals carry. Direct broadcast satellite signals are expressly excluded from the scope of the convention.

Copyright issues are also raised by the development of direct broadcast satellite technology. Direct broadcast satellites (DBSs) can be used to broadcast directly into individual home receivers. In that type of transmission, the organization that produces the program also broadcasts it. Although it is clear that on the earth's surface existing copyright laws will apply, it is difficult to coordinate the licensing requirements of copyrighted work to be broadcast to different countries. The distinction between who is the originator and who is actually conducting a transmission, and when a public performance of the protected work occurs, may blur.[40]

It is likely that protection mechanisms for copyrighted works in the context of satellite transmission will be refined as the technology in the field advances. In addition to WIPO, UNESCO and other United Nations bodies, including the Committee on the Peaceful Uses of Outer Space (COPUOS), maintain an interest in the effects of broadcast technology on intellectual property rights. At the international organization level, however, the issue of intellectual property rights is intertwined with considerations of human rights and state sovereignty. Even COPUOS and its Legal Subcommittee, which have dealt for many years with direct broadcast satellite issues, have not really focused on property rights protection but on questions of "free flow" of information and the rights of states to restrict that flow.[41]

INDUSTRIAL PROPERTY RIGHTS

The laws of industrial property confer certain exclusive rights on what are described as the proprietors of industrial property. Those rights are normally granted following registration of certain precisely defined categories of technology. As we have seen, patent rights are granted with respect to inventions or designs that demonstrate a certain level of novelty and that have an industrial application. Trademark rights are conferred in respect of trade symbols that serve to distinguish the products of an applicant's business. Industrial property rights are similar to those arising under know-how agreements, except that industrial rights result from specific acts of technological inventiveness, whereas know-how agreements tend to involve the more general application of technology in a commercial situation. Know-how, therefore, includes the knowledge of the organization, management, marketing techniques, and operating procedures of a commercial enterprise.[42] Within the general conceptual heading of industrial property rights, mention should be made of two international agreements.

The Hague Agreement Concerning the Deposit of Industrial Designs of 1925 operates within the framework of the mentioned Paris Convention. An industrial design deposited with the International Bureau of WIPO is afforded protection within all members of the Hague Union, without the necessity for national registration, unless specifically required by the law of a member state. The owner of an international deposit enjoys the priority right afforded to members of the Paris Convention.

The Locarno Agreement Establishing an International Classification for Industrial Designs came into force on April 27, 1970. It establishes a system of classification for industrial design for use by the industrial property offices of the world.[43]

NASA PATENT WAIVERS

In implementing the provisions of Section 305 (f) of the *National Aeronautics and Space Act of 1958*, as amended,[44] and the *Presidential Memorandum and Statement of Government Patent Policy to the Heads of the Executive Departments and Agencies* of February, 1983, the government will, under certain circumstances, waive the rights of the United States in inventions made in the performance of work under NASA contracts. Among the most important goals of the policy are to provide incentives to foster inventiveness and encourage the reporting of inventions made under NASA contracts; to provide for the widest possible dissemination of new technology resulting from NASA programs; and to provide early utilization, expeditious development, and continued availability of this new technology for commercial purposes and the public benefit.

The NASA Inventions and Contributions Board will normally recommend grant of a request for advance waiver of domestic rights submitted prior to execution of a contract in one of the following situations:

1. when the contractor is not located in the United States or is subject to the control of a foreign government;
2. when a determination has been made by government authority authorized to conduct foreign intelligence or counterintelligence activities that the restriction or elimination of the right to retain title to inventions made in the performance of work is necessary to protect the security of such activities; or
3. where the Board finds that exceptional circumstances exist, such that restriction or elimination of the right to retain title will promote one of the following objectives:
   i. promoting the utilization of inventions arising from federally supported research and development,
   ii. encouraging maximum participation of industry in federally supported research and development,
   iii. ensuring that inventions are used in a manner to promote free competition and enterprise, and
   iv. promoting the commercialization and public availability of inventions made in the United States by U.S. business and labor.[45]

An advance waiver, when granted, will apply only to the inventions reported to NASA under the applicable terms of the contract and a designation made within six months, or a reasonable time thereafter, that the contractor elects title to the invention and intends to file or has filed a U.S. patent application. The waiver extends to the invention claimed in any patent application filed on the reported invention, including any subsequent continuation application thereof, provided the claims of the subsequent application do not substantially change the scope of the reported invention.[46] When a specified invention has been reported to NASA and waiver of rights has not been granted, the board will normally recommend grant of a waiver of domestic rights to such invention if the request is received within eight months of first disclosure to NASA.[47]

The board will consider the waiver of foreign rights in any designated country with the waiver of domestic rights when so requested. The board will also consider a separate request for foreign rights. Waivers of foreign rights are normally granted unless the board finds that the economic interests of the United States will not be served by it or if NASA has determined, prior to the request, to file a patent application in the designated country.[48]

Any invention for which waiver of domestic or foreign rights has been granted is subject to the reservation by the administrator of an irrevocable, nonexclusive, nontransferable, royalty-free license for the practice of the invention throughout the world by or on behalf of the United States or any foreign government pursuant to any treaty or agreement with the United States. In certain cases, NASA also reserves the right to require the contractor, an assignee, or exclusive licensee of the invention to grant a license to an applicant or to grant the license itself. NASA will do so in the following cases:

1. such action is necessary because the contractor or assignee has not taken, or is not expected to take effective steps to achieve practical application of the invention;
2. such action is necessary to alleviate health or safety needs that are not reasonably satisfied by the contractor, assignee, or licensees;
3. such action is necessary to meet specified requirements for public use that are not being reasonably satisfied by the contractor; or
4. such action is necessary because the agreement required by the preference for U.S. industry has not been obtained or because a licensee of the exclusive right to use or sell any invention in the United States is in breach of such agreement.

Each contractor reporting an invention is granted a revocable, nonexclusive, royalty-free license in each patent application filed in any country on the invention and in any resulting patent in which the government acquires title. The license extends to the contractor's domestic subsidiaries and affiliates, if any, within the corporate structure of which the contractor is a party and includes the right to grant sublicenses of the same scope to the extent the contractor was legally obligated to do so at the time the contract was awarded. The license and right are transferable only with the approval of the administrator except when transferred to the successor of that part of the contractor's business to which the invention pertains.

LICENSING OF NASA INVENTIONS

As was noted earlier, it is the policy of the U.S. government to use the patent system to promote the utilization of inventions arising from NASA supported research and development. NASA inventions are therefore made available for licensing as deemed appropriate in the public interest. NASA may grant nonexclusive, partially exclusive, or exclusive licenses on inventions in its custody. The following restrictions apply:[49]

1. A license may be granted only if the applicant has supplied NASA with a satisfactory plan for development or marketing of the invention, and with information about the applicant's capability to fulfill the plan.
2. A license granting rights to use or sell under a NASA invention in the United States is normally granted only to a licensee who agrees that any products embodying the invention will be manufactured substantially in the United States.

Among the requirements of the license is that the licensee carry out the plan for development or marketing of the invention to bring the invention to practical application within a period specified in the license and to continue to make the benefits of the invention reasonably accessible to the public.

NOTES

1. See Barbara Luxemberg and Gerald J. Mossinghoff, *Intellectual Property and Space Activities*, 13 Journal of Space Law 1, 1985, pp. 8 *et seq.*

2. Raymond E. Vickery, Jr., *The Laws and Outer Space: Intellectual Property*, 4 Journal of Law and Technology, 1989, p. 10.

3. *Id.*, p. 11.

4. For a full discussion of trademark protection, see Michael Blakeney, *Legal Aspects of the Transfer of Technology to Developing Countries*, ESC Publishing Limited, Oxford, 1989.

5. Vickery, *supra*, at 10.

6. Rachel B. Trinder, *Why New Federal Legislation Is an Important Development for Both the Space Community and the Space Bar*, 38 Federal Bar News and Journal, 1991, p. 396.

7. See John F. Kohler, *Space Pharmaceuticals: Will the United States Fumble Another High Technology Industry?* 58 Journal of Air Law and Commerce 2, Winter 1992, pp. 511 *et seq.*

8. David Osborne, *Business in Space*, Atlantic Monthly, May 1985, at 45–53, 56–58.

9. Opened for signature on January 27, 1967, and entered into force on October 10, 1967.

10. Agreement on the Rescue of Astronauts, the Return of Astronauts and the Return of Objects Launched into Outer Space, entered into force December 3, 1968.

11. Convention on International Liability for Damage Caused by Space Objects, entered into force October 9, 1973.

12. Convention on the Registration of Objects Launched into Outer Space, entered into force September 15, 1976.

13. Agreement Governing the Activities of States on the Moon and Other Celestial Bodies, entered into force July 11, 1984.

14. Pikus, *Law and Security in Outer Space: Private Sector Interests*, 11 Journal of Space Law, 1983, pp. 112–113.

15. See Luxemberg and Mossinghoff, *supra*, p. 10.

16. See Blakeney, *supra*, at 17.

17. *Id.*, at 17–18.

18. Kohler, *supra*, p. 540.

19. 35 U.S.C. § 112 (1988), in Kohler, *supra*, at 541.

20. Kohler, *supra*, at 541.

21. 35 U.S.C. §100(c) (1988).

22. Deepsouth Packing Co. v. The Laitram Corp., 406 U.S. 518 (1972).

23. Pub. Law 98–622 (1984).

24. 35 U.S.C. § 105 (Supp. 1991).

25. Rep. No. 266, 101st Cong. 2nd. Sess. 5 (1990).

26. See Kohler, *supra*, at 548.

27. See Saipan v. Department of the Interior, 502 F.2d 90, 97 (9th Cir. 1974).

28. Id., in Kohler, *supra*, at 549.

29. See Kohler, *supra*, at 552–553.

30. *Id.*, *supra*, see note No. 182.

31. Convention for the Establishment of a European Space Research Organization, OFS 14 June, 1962, EIF 20 March, 1964, *Basic Texts of the European Space Agency*, Vol. I, Conventions and Rules, part A1/1.

32. See Andrew Young, *Law and Policy in the Space Stations' Era*, Martinus Nijhoff Publishers, Dardrecht, 1989, at 174–175.

33. Convention for the Establishment of a European Organisation for the Development and Construction of Space Vehicle Launchers, OFS March 29, 1962, EIF February 29, 1964.

34. *Id.*, article 8(1)(c),(d).

35. *Id.*, art. 8(1)(e)(i) & (2).

36. See Kallenbach and Osterlinck, *The Evolution of the Agency's Patent Policy*, ESA Bulletin No. 44, November 1985, in Young, *supra* at 176.

37. *Id.*

38. See Luxemberg and Mossinghoff, *supra*, at 10.

39. Universal Copyright Convention (Paris, 1971); Berne Convention for the Protection of Literary Works (Paris, 1971).

40. See Luxemberg and Mossinghoff, *supra*, at 12.

41. *Id.*

42. See Blakeney, *supra*, at 5.

43. *Ibid.*, at 20.

44. 42 U.S.C. 2457 (f).

45. 14 CFR Ch. V, 1245.104.

46. *Id.*

47. 14 CFR Ch. V, 1245.105.
48. 14 CFR Ch. V, 1245.106.
49. 14 CFR Ch. V, 1245.204.

Chapter Eleven

Technology Transfer and Spinoffs

The transfer of technology, particularly in the aerospace field, that may benefit the economy of the United States at a time of defense cutbacks and economic recession, is one of those subjects that is much talked about. The topic, however, is a most complex one and it encompasses many government and private activities, different or even contradictory government policies, and laws and regulations both national and international. The notion of technology transfer can be rather confusing simply because of the many definitions involved, with different people understanding the concept to mean different things. Technology may be transmitted in a passive way, where the user actively pursues the technology or idea. In this type of situation, information can be disseminated through scientific publications, technology exhibitions, information networks, and other such means. Active transfer, on the other hand, is done through a direct and specific transaction or program.[1]

Even if the definitions of all the activities involved in technology transfer were clearly understood, there still remain distinctions that divide this field into several different branches. Technology can be transferred from one private firm to another. It can be transferred from the federal or state government to one or more private companies or to a certain class of users such as small businesses. Or it can be developed and adapted to a different use, such as dual use technology, which the government makes available for commercial exploitation. Sometimes, sophisticated inventions or developments can be reapplied to uses different—often remotely so—from the original application, giving rise to the spinoff phenomenon. Certain types of technology are sometimes transferred to other nations, usually developing countries.

Every sector of technology transfer has its set of rules and challenges. Transactions between private entities involve negotiations and contracts; government originated technology usually involves some form of competitive bidding; international transfer almost always raises issues of national security and export controls. The transfer of technology, however, and particularly that resulting from aerospace research, is a very important activity. It provides a substantial return on the national research investment in terms of contribution to the economy, job production, industrial productivity, lifestyle innovations, and solution to problems of everyday life.

UNITED STATES LEGISLATION AND POLICY DESIGNED TO PROMOTE DOMESTIC TECHNOLOGY TRANSFER

At the U.S. level, much has been done to disseminate that technology that is not critical to the national security of the country. Section 203(a)(3) of the *NASA Act* requires NASA to "provide for the widest practicable and appropriate dissemination of information concerning its activities and the results thereof." The *Freedom of Information Act* allows requestors to obtain access to the records of government agencies, including NASA, unless an exception applies.[2] One of the exceptions regards the protection of trade secrets and confidential business information entrusted to NASA. With respect to launch services agreements, for example, the purchaser of launch services and the entity collaborating may mark the data furnished with a notice labeling such data a trade secret. Following are some of the most important statutes that have a bearing or a substantial effect on the transfer of technology.

The *Stevenson-Wydler Technology Innovation Act of 1980*[3] established and funded Offices of Research and Technology applications at major laboratories to identify information on technologies and provide that information to private industry, universities and state and local governments. The *Bayh-Dole University and Small Business Patent Procedure Act of 1980* allowed small firms and universities to obtain title to inventions funded by the federal government.

The *Small Business Innovation and Development Act of 1982*[4] mandated that federal agencies develop small business innovation research programs and establish specific goals to help small business and minority, disadvantaged organizations participate in contracts, grants, and cooperative research and development agreements (CRDAs). The declaration of policy of section 638 states that:

Research and development are major factors in the growth and progress of industry and the national economy. The expense of carrying on research and development programs is beyond the means of many small business concerns, and such concerns are handicapped in obtaining the benefits of research and development programs conducted at Government expense. These small business concerns are thereby placed at a competitive disadvantage. This weakens the competitive free enterprise system and prevents the orderly development of the national economy. It is the policy of the government that assistance be given to small business concerns to enable them to undertake and to obtain the benefits of research and development in order to maintain and strengthen the competitive free enterprise system and the national economy.

Among the duties of the administration with regard to assistance to small business concerns are

1. to assist small business concerns to obtain government contracts for research and development;
2. to assist small business concerns to obtain the benefits of research and development performed under government contracts or at government expense;
3. to develop and maintain a source file and an information program to ensure each qualified and interested small business concern the opportunity to participate in federal agency small business innovation research programs;
4. to coordinate with participating agencies a schedule for release of Small Business Innovation Research (SBIR) solicitations, and to prepare a master release schedule so as to maximize small businesses' opportunities to respond to solicitations; and
5. to independently survey and monitor the operation of SBIR programs within participating federal agencies.

Pursuant to the act, the administrator is authorized to consult with representatives of small business concerns in order to assist and encourage such firms to undertake joint programs for research and development carried out through such corporate or other mechanism as may be most appropriate for the purpose. Such joint programs may include the following purposes:

1. to construct, acquire, or establish laboratories and other facilities for the conduct of research;
2. to undertake and utilize applied research;
3. to collect research information related to a particular industry and disseminate it to participating members;

4. to conduct applied research on a protected, proprietary, and contractual basis with member or nonmember firms, government agencies and others;
5. to prosecute applications for patents and render patent services for participating members; and
6. to negotiate and grant licenses under patents held under the joint program, and to establish corporations designed to exploit particular patents obtained by it.

The *National Cooperative Research Act of 1984*[5] permitted registered consortia to engage in joint R&D ventures without violating antitrust laws. The *National Defense Authorization Act of 1987*[6] encouraged the secretary of defense to promote domestic technology transfer of DoD-developed technology to the extent consistent with national security objectives. The act also called for the secretary of defense to examine and implement methods for DoD personnel to promote technology transfer. *Executive Order 12591, Facilitating Access to Science and Technology*[7] called on the secretary of defense to identify new technologies that could be useful to U.S. industries and universities and to accelerate efforts to make new technologies more readily accessible to those users.

The *Omnibus Trade and Competitiveness Act of 1988*[8] changed the name of the National Bureau of Standards to the National Institute of Standards and Technology (NIST) to reflect NIST's broadened role of promoting the commercialization of federally developed technology and to transfer that technology to universities, private industry, and state and local governments. The act also created regional centers for the transfer of manufacturing technologies, made provisions to assist state technology extension programs, and established a clearinghouse for state and local initiatives on productivity, technology, and innovation.[9] The policy statement of the act notes, in part, that:

1. the fundamental research and related education programs supported by the federal government and conducted by the nation's universities and colleges are essential to our national security, and to our health, economic welfare, and general well-being;
2. many national research and related education programs conducted by universities and colleges are now hindered by obsolete research buildings and equipment, and many institutions lack sufficient resources to repair, renovate, or replace their laboratories;
3. the nation's capacity to conduct high-quality research and education programs and to maintain its competitive position at the forefront of modern science, engineering, and technology is threatened by this research capital deficit, which

poses serious and adverse consequences to our future national security, health, welfare, and ability to compete in the international marketplace;

4. a national effort to spur reinvestment in research facilities is needed, and national, state, and local policies and cooperative programs are required that will yield maximum return on the investment of scarce national resources and sustain a commitment to excellence in research and education; and
5. the National Science Foundation, as part of its responsibility for maintaining the vitality of the nation's academic research, and in partnership with the states, industry, and universities and colleges must assist in enhancing the historic linkages between federal investment in academic research and training and investment in the research capital base by reinvesting in the capital facilities that modern research and education programs require.

The *Federal Technology Transfer Acts of 1986 and 1989*[10] created the CRDAs to promote commercialization of technology by turning federal scientists and private firms into joint participants on selected projects. Under this legislation, which took most federal laboratories about 18 months to put into effect, the government can waive intellectual property rights in favor of the participating company, grant an industrial partner an exclusive license to the technology, authorize individual laboratory directors to make deals of cooperation with industry, and give federal employees a share of the royalties earned on their patented inventions. With few exceptions, before 1986, what the government created, the government owned.

The act[11] establishes the Office of Industrial Technology, whose director has a duty to

1. determine the relationships of technological developments and international technology transfers to the output, employment, productivity, and world trade performance of United States and foreign industrial sectors;
2. determine the influence of economic, labor, and other conditions, industrial structure and management, and government policies on technological developments in particular industrial sectors worldwide;
3. identify technological needs, problems, and opportunities within and across industrial sectors that, if addressed, could make a significant contribution to the economy of the United States;
4. assess whether the capital, technical, and other resources being allocated to domestic industrial sectors that are likely to generate new technologies are adequate to meet private and social demands for goods and services and to promote productivity and economic growth;

5. propose and support studies and policy experiments, in cooperation with other federal agencies, to determine the effectiveness of measures with the potential of advancing U.S. technological innovation;
6. provide that cooperative efforts to stimulate industrial innovation be undertaken between the director and other officials in the Department of Commerce responsible for such areas as trade and economic assistance; and
7. consider government measures with the potential of advancing U.S. technological innovation and exploiting innovations of foreign origin.

The objective of the Centers for Industrial Technology established by the act is to enhance technological innovation through

a. the participation of individuals from industry and universities in cooperative technological innovation activities;
b. the development of the generic research base, important for technological advance and innovative activity, in which individual firms have little incentive to invest, but that may have significant economic or strategic importance, such as manufacturing technology;
c. the education and training of individuals in the technological innovation process;
d. the improvement of mechanisms for the dissemination of scientific, engineering, and technical information among university and industry;
e. the utilization of the capability and expertise, where appropriate, that exist in federal laboratories; and
f. the development of continuing financial support from other mission agencies, from state and local government, and from industry and universities through, among other means, fees, licenses, and royalties.[12]

Among the activities of the Centers envisaged by the act are:

1. research supportive of technological and industrial innovation including cooperative industry-university basic and applied research;
2. assistance to individuals and small businesses in the generation, evaluation, and development of technological ideas supportive of industrial innovation and new business ventures;
3. technical assistance and advisory services to industry, particularly small businesses; and
4. curriculum development, training, and instruction in invention, entrepreneurship, and industrial innovation.

To promote technological innovation and commercialization of research and development efforts, each center has the option of acquiring title to any invention conceived or made under the auspices of the center that was supported at least in part by federal funds, provided that

a. the center reports the invention to the supporting agency together with a list of each country in which the center elects to file a patent application on the invention;
b. said option is exercised at the time of disclosure of invention or within such time thereafter as may be provided in the grant or cooperative agreement;
c. the center intends to promote the commercialization of the invention and file a U.S. patent application;
d. royalties be used for compensation of the inventor or for educational or research activities of the center;
e. the center make periodic reports to the supporting agency, and the supporting agency may treat information contained in such reports as privileged and confidential technical, commercial, and financial information and not subject to disclosures under the *Freedom of Information Act*; and
f. any federal department or agency shall have the royalty-free right to practice, or have practiced on its behalf, the invention for governmental purposes.

The supporting agency retains the right to acquire title to any patent on an invention in any country in which the center elects not to file a patent application or fails to file within a reasonable time. Where a center has retained title to an invention, the supporting agency has the right to require the center or its licensee to grant a nonexclusive, partially exclusive, or exclusive license to a responsible applicant, on terms that are reasonable under the circumstances, if the supporting agency determines, after public notice that such action is necessary

1. because the center or licensee has not taken and is not expected to take timely and effective action to achieve practical application of the invention;
2. to meet health, safety, environmental, or national security needs, which are not reasonably satisfied by the contractor or licensee; or
3. because the granting of exclusive rights in the invention has tended substantially to lessen competition or to result in undue market concentration in the United States in any line of commerce to which the technology relates.

The law also requires the establishment of Research and Technology Applications Offices within each federal laboratory.[13] The functions of those offices are to (a) prepare an application assessment of each research and development project in which the laboratory is engaged that has potential for successful application in state or local government or in private industry; (b) provide and disseminate information on federally owned or originated products, processes, and services, having potential application to state and local governments and to private industry; (c) cooperate with and assist the Center for the Utilization of Federal Technology and other organizations that link the research and development resources of that laboratory and the federal government as a whole to potential users in state and local government and private industry; and (d) provide technical assistance in response to requests from state and local government officials. The Office of Research and Technology Applications and similar organizational structures are forbidden to substantially compete with similar services available in the private sector.

Another institution worth mentioning in this context is the Center for the Utilization of Federal Technology.[14] The functions of the center are to (1) serve as a central clearinghouse for the collection, dissemination, and transfer of information on federally owned or originated technologies having potential application to state and local governments and to private industry; (2) coordinate the activities of the Offices of Research and Technology Applications of the federal laboratories; (3) utilize the expertise and services of the National Science Foundation and the existing Federal Laboratory Consortium for Technology Transfer; (4) receive requests for technical assistance from state and local governments and refer these requests to the appropriate federal laboratories; (5) provide funding, at the discretion of the secretary, for federal laboratories to provide the assistance entrusted to them; and (6) use appropriate technology transfer mechanisms such as personnel exchanges and computer-based systems.

In the 1989 version of the *Federal Technology Transfer Act* (FTTA), Congress added economic competitiveness as a laboratory mission, established mechanisms for swift and predictable creation of cooperative research arrangements, and provided for the protection of intellectual property created in such ventures. The trend toward such cooperative R&D and technology transfer has received wide support. For example, a 1991 report by the Washington-based Center for Strategic and International Studies Steering Committee on Security and Technology[15] urged the government "to implement more fully the provisions of the *Stevenson-Wydler Technology Innovation Act* and the *Federal Technology Transfer Acts of 1986 and 1989*, which mandate greater efforts to transfer technology from the public to the private sector." The committee also proposed that Congress enact legislation to make cooperative industry-laboratory R&D ventures in critical technologies an explicit mission of the federal and national laboratories to help reverse the downward trend in U.S. international competitiveness.[16]

NIST, which has been in the business of working cooperatively with industry for a long time, has had no trouble adjusting to FTTA legislation. The impact of the technology transfer has been to improve the government's ability to negotiate intellectual property rights for technology as part of a cooperative R&D agreement. Companies are apparently beginning to overcome the general prejudice of working with federal laboratories, in part because of the streamlined CRDA process. At many labs it takes only 60 days to negotiate CRDAs, versus six months for predecessor agreements.[17] Another reason for the popularity of these programs is the economic recession, which discourages unnecessary capital expenditures. Companies can go to a federal laboratory to conduct research and not go through the capital investment on their own to do it. In the negotiation of CRDAs, as far as the legal requirements are concerned, small and large companies are on equal footing because Congress wrote the law specifically to assist small businesses.

Forty-two Army laboratories have established Offices of Research and Technology Applications (ORTAs) since 1988, when the technology transfer legislation was implemented. Today, the Army boasts 172 CRDAs, most involving small companies, which tend to be more flexible and entrepreneurial than larger companies. As part of its CRDA program, the DoD issued a regulation that makes it uniform across the services to pay military inventors 20 percent of royalties, or $1,000 on each royalty payment, whichever is higher.[18] Another successful strategy for the Army is an initiative that calls for formal cooperation between the Army's technology transfer program and its SBIR program, a three-phase effort to help small companies fund novel technologies and develop products. Small companies also constitute the majority of the Navy's 12 operational CRDAs and another dozen or so in the negotiation stage.[19]

SPINOFFS

In aerospace design, every subsystem must be very efficient and reliable, yet as small and light as technology permits—requirements that are shared by many types of medical devices. That is one reason why the field of health and medicine has been a particular beneficiary of aerospace spinoff. The United States leads the world in the technology of building complete and reliable aerospace systems in incredibly tiny packages and that technology has spawned a line of life-saving medical adaptations. An example is the cooperative development of human-implantable systems by a group of research organizations and medical equipment manufacturers who applied such space technologies as advanced long-life batteries, microminiaturized components, electronic sensors, and telemetry, the wireless relay of coded signals for high volume two-way communication between earth and orbit. Some of the results have been a rechargeable cardiac pacemaker that eliminates the recurring need for surgery to replace batteries, an advanced heart pacer that may be reprogrammed without surgery via biotelemetry, and an automatic implantable "defibrillator" that senses the start of fibrillation—in which the heart loses its ability to pump blood—and corrects it by sending an electrical impulse to the heart.[20]

For the exploration of the Moon, astronauts needed a compact, lightweight, battery-powered, long-use drill to extract core samples from beneath the lunar surface. Under NASA contract, a company developed one, then used the technology to produce a line of cordless tools for consumer, industrial, and medical use. Available to airport, municipal, and industrial firefighters is a bayonet-type spray nozzle, developed for Shuttle landing emergencies, that can be thrust through the skin of a transportation vehicle or certain building material to deliver extinguishants to the interior. A sophisticated smoke/fire detection system used in the Skylab manned spacecraft provided the technology for a home use detection device.[21] The list goes on and on with countless other examples of technology transfer that highlight the importance of spinoff in the aerospace field.

At the direction of Congress, in April 1991 NASA initiated a five-year development program to establish the National Technology Transfer Center (NTTC) as a national resource for federal technology transfer. The NTTC's principal mission is to assist all federal agencies in executing the federal-wide technology transfer mandate as a means to enhancing U.S. competitiveness. The NTTC serves as a "hub" for the network, providing core capabilities and cross-cutting services that accelerate and expand the transfer of federal technologies to the U.S. private sector.[22] The NTTC is establishing key capabilities and services to (a) serve as the national clearinghouse for federal technology transfer, linking U.S. firms and industry with federal agencies and laboratories, the Regional Technology Transfer Centers, and state and local agencies and (b) to provide training and education services to government and industry to develop the individual skills and organizational approaches critical to technology transfer.[23]

The Regional Technology Transfer Centers (RTTCs), established in six regions spanning the United States, began operations in January 1992. The new centers, which replaced NASA's longstanding network of Industrial Applications Centers, reflect NASA's initiative to upgrade and restructure its technology transfer program. The regional deployment, aligned with the six Federal Laboratory Consortium regions and covering all 50 states, allows the centers to work closely with a wide range of federal, state, and local programs in serving the technology and related business needs of industry in each region. The RTTCs also utilize the NTTC and the national network to access technologies from throughout the federal R&D base and link together additional capabilities and services from the NTTC and others across the United States. The services provided by the RTTCs include computerized searches of federal technology data bases; assessment of technology requirements; analysis of technology applications and engineering reports; and commercialization services such as technology brokering, business analyses, and venture capital sourcing.

The Ballistic Missile Defense Organization (BMDO), formerly known as the Strategic Defense Initiative Organization (SDIO), has been involved for some time in the transfer of technology. The Technology Applications Office of that organization has formed a working agreement with the National Technology Transfer Center. Under the agreement, the NTTC will operate the Technology Applications Information System (TAIS)—BMDO's on-line technology transfer data base—and provide other technology transfer and commercialization support. This includes producing publications on technology transfer by BMDO, assisting BMDO contractors with commercialization through technology applications reviews, and providing a liaison with professional and trade organizations, government programs, and other interested parties.[24]

INTERNATIONAL TRANSFER OF TECHNOLOGY

The International Agencies

The World Intellectual Property Organization was established by a convention signed at Stockholm in 1967, which entered into force in 1970. On December 17, 1974, WIPO became a specialized agency of the United Nations. WIPO was established to promote the protection of intellectual property throughout the world through cooperation among states and to ensure administrative cooperation among the organizations previously established to afford protection of intellectual property. Those organizations are

a. the Paris Union, officially the International Union for the Protection of Industrial Property, which is composed by those states that are parties to the Paris Convention of 1883, as amended in 1967, and

b. the Berne Union, officially the International Union for the Protection of Literary and Artistic Works. It is composed of state parties to a convention concluded in Berne in 1886 and revised in 1967.

The basic responsibilities of WIPO are registration activities, the promotion of intergovernmental cooperation in the administration of intellectual property, and specialized program activities. In 1975, WIPO began its Program for Patent Information and Documentation, by which it provides, free of charge, search reports on institutions in developing countries.[25] WIPO has also had a role in the establishment of a patent information and document center (CADIB) within the framework of the African Intellectual Property Organization (OAPI) to serve the needs of French speaking African countries, and a similar information and document center (ESAPADIC) within the framework of the Industrial Property Organization for English Speaking countries of Africa (ESARIPO).[26]

WIPO's role in the transfer of technology to developing countries consists for the most part of its development assistance programs. Such assistance takes three forms: (a) educational assistance both to induce familiarity with the concept of intellectual and industrial property and for the training of government officials, (b) assistance to developing countries in the drafting of appropriate legislation, and (c) assistance in establishing the appropriate administrative infrastructure.

The first session of the United Nations Conference on Trade and Development (UNCTAD) met at Geneva in 1964 when the General Assembly established UNCTAD as one of its organs. Its basic functions are to

a. promote international trade, particularly between countries at different stages of development, with a view to accelerating the economic growth of developing countries;

b. formulate and implement principles and policies on international trade and related problems of economic development;

c. review and facilitate the coordination of activities of other institutions within the UN system in the field of international trade and related problems of economic development and in this regard to cooperate with the assembly and the Economic and Social Council (ECOSOC) in respect of the performance of their charter responsibilities for coordination;

d. initiate action for the negotiation and adoption of multilateral legal instruments in the field of trade; and

e. act as a center for harmonization of trade and related development policies of governments and regional economic groups.[27]

An Intergovernmental Working Group was established in 1970 as an organ of UNCTAD to begin work on a draft code of conduct for the transfer of technology. The working group eventually became the Standing Committee on Transfer of Technology, which in 1976 established the Advisory Service on Transfer and Development of Technology (ASTT). The functions of ASTT include:

1. the preparation of national technology policies and plans and their implementation in coordination with other relevant economic policies and plans;
2. the establishment of national centers for the transfer and development of technology;
3. the establishment of regional centers for the transfer and development of technology and of appropriate linkages between them;
4. dealing with the technoeconomic and developmental aspects of technological information;
5. the evaluation of economic and developmental aspects of technological information;
6. the establishment of training programs dealing with the transfer of technology.[28]

Several other international organizations have dealt, on occasion, with the transfer of technology. The United Nations Industrial Development Organization (UNIDO), for example, in 1973 issued a licensing guide by the title of "Guidelines for the Acquisition of Foreign Technology in Developing Countries with Special Reference to Technology Licensing Agreements," which was revised in 1979.[29] UNIDO also administers a Technical Information Exchange System, which provides data on terms and conditions of licensing, know-how, and technical assistance agreements entered into by developing countries participating in the system. One of the main objectives of UNIDO is to strengthen the negotiating position of developing countries by highlighting technology options and facilitating the establishment of technological priorities and indigenous development.[30]

ECOSOC was established in 1974 to study the interrelationships of transnational corporations with developing countries. The United Nations Conference on Science and Technology for Development (UNCSTD) began in 1979 its activities to promote the cultural and technological independence of developing countries.[31]

Technology Transfer Techniques

As we have seen in previous chapters, most inventions and technological developments are protected by various categories of intellectual or industrial property. A clear understanding of those concepts is imperative to have a full grasp of the problems involved in technology transfer. The most important types of intellectual property are the following.[32]

Patents. A basic patent is essentially a statutory privilege granted by the government to an inventor for a set number of years, to exclude other persons from manufacturing, using, or selling the product protected by the patent. Additions to or improvements of patents may themselves be the subject of a patent and generally considered to be completely independent from the original patent. In some countries, it is possible to obtain limited protection for certain objects of utility that embody a more limited technological advance than what is usually required for patentability. These patents are known as petty patents or utility models.

Patents of Importation. Patent rights in some jurisdictions may be obtained to permit the local exploitation of foreign inventions. The advantage of this type of patent is that technology can be imported without the constraints of the novelty requirement.

Technovation Certificates. "Technovation" is defined by Section 501 of the *WIPO Model Law on Inventions for Developing Countries*[33] as a "solution to a specific problem in the field of technology, proposed by an employee of an enterprise . . . for use by that enterprise, and which relates to the activities of the enterprise but which, on the date of the proposal, has not been used or actively considered for use by the enterprise." The WIPO Model Law provides for cooperation between an employee and the company as well as the method for employee remuneration.

Transfer of Technology Patent. The WIPO Model Law proposes the creation of this type of patent in order to encourage foreign patent owners to seek registration and to work patented inventions in developing countries. An application for this type of patent must be jointly filed by the foreign owner of the patent and the domestic partner who is going to exploit the invention in the developing country.

Industrial Designs. Section 2 of the WIPO Model Law defines industrial design as "any composition of lines or colors or any three-dimensional form, whether or not associated with lines or colors . . . provided that such composition or form gives a special appearance to a product of industry or handicraft and can serve as a pattern for a product of industry or handicraft."

Trademarks. A trademark is a sign that serves to distinguish the product of one enterprise from the products of others.

Know-how and Trade Secrets. Know-how is the way in which technology is applied in a commercial situation.

Keeping in mind these intellectual rights, which can obviously place limitations on the transfer of technology, and other obstacles that are discussed later, a brief description is in order of the actual methods for the transfer of technology. The chief method for the international transfer of technology is a commercial transaction between enterprises or institutions in different countries. The selection of the modalities of the specific arrangement depends on a variety of considerations. Financial considerations, laws and regulations of the recipient country, the complexity of the technology involved and other factors play a significant role.[34]

If the technology to be acquired is very specific, a purchase or license contract is normally adequate. Where the transfer involves the establishment of a manufacturing structure, however, many transactions become necessary. They may include feasibility studies, contracts for the purchase and financing of equipment, the design and construction of the works, preparation and inviting of tenders, evaluation of bids, agreements for the training and management, erection of the plant and installation of equipment, service agreements, and many other arrangements.[35]

One of the main characteristics of intellectual property rights is the right of the owner of the relevant property rights to assign them. The assignee, or purchaser, acquires all the rights of the vendor (assignor) to the relevant piece of intellectual or industrial property. Commercial transfer of technology often involves said assignment. The assignment of rights is usually done in exchange for the payment of a lump sum. Alternatively, a license agreement can be used in which property rights can be purchased through the periodic payment of royalties over the productive life of the technology involved.

The licensing of intellectual or industrial property rights and know-how is the most common way of acquiring technology. In that type of arrangement, the owner of intellectual rights or know-how, the licensor, grants permission to use those rights and information for a sum of money or other benefit. He is thus spared the trouble and expense of manufacturing and marketing the goods and services derived from the industrial property rights, particularly where the goods or services are to be sold in another country or territory. By exploiting local knowledge, business contacts, and expertise of a foreign licensee, the licensor may be able to avoid some of the complicated problems of operating in a foreign environment. The advantages for the licensee include the acquisition of a developed and tested industrial process without the risks, expenses, and delay of its development.[36] In some developing countries, the unavailability of facilities and resources for R&D, particularly in a field such as aerospace, often makes the licensing of foreign technology rights the only way to obtaining them.

Although a detailed description of provisions in a licensing agreement is beyond the scope and purpose of this chapter, a brief mention of the basic concepts is in order and is provided next.[37]

— Grant-back provisions require that a licensee transfer to the licensor any improvements in the technology involved.

— Restrictions after the expiration of industrial property rights are designed to limit the benefit accruing to the licensor after he is no longer entitled to the exclusive use of the registered rights. Exceptions to these types of provisions include the payment of installments of a lump sum.

— No-challenge provisions prevent a licensee from challenging the validity of a licensed industrial property right.

— Tying and appointment of personnel provisions require that the licensee purchase additional plant and machinery or raw materials, or hire personnel designated by the licensor. The imposition of a tie of this type may be justified as a necessity for the successful operation and exploitation of technology.

— Noncompetition and price-fixing conditions often impose direct or indirect restraints on the activities of the licensee. Direct restraints typically prevent the licensee from manufacturing or selling products that compete with those of the licensor. Indirect restraints include clauses that forbid licensees from dealing with competitors of the licensor or require them to get their service requirements or raw materials from the licensor. Price fixing usually relates to the way in which the products or services are to be priced and marketed. The licensor may specify prices to be charged or set minimum prices. Generally, price fixing is considered objectionable as anticompetitive. It is less objectionable, however, if the restrictions are posed exclusively and unilaterally by the licensor on a vertical basis as opposed to an agreement between technology providers.

— Export restrictions are designed to protect the licensor's business in those countries where he trades from the competition of its licensees. Developing countries do not favor this type of arrangement but in most cases accept it as a condition of acquiring the technology.

— Field-of-use clauses confine the license to a specific field of application where the technology may be applicable in different fields.

— Exclusivity is given by a provision by which a licensor grants the license on an exclusive basis or reserves the right to use the technology itself or to grant it to third parties.

— Territory is often specified in a license in order to confine the right to use the technology to a certain area.

Licensing is only one of the many arrangements involved in the transfer of technology. The overall picture is usually more complex and may involve the supply of raw materials, equipment, labor, and marketing assistance. A common type of arrangement is the so-called turn-key contract, which provides for the construction of an industrial complex in accordance with a design and incorporating technology to be selected and supplied by a single contractor. Where the purchaser operates as a general, supervising contractor with a number of contractors providing different aspects of the works, separate contracts are negotiated.[38]

Another method used in the transfer of technology is the joint venture. The joint activity may include the manufacture of products, the provision of services, or even research and development. The typical arrangement works by a developing country participant supplying the raw materials and personnel and the other participant providing the industrial property rights and know-how and capital equipment. The joint venture as an entity takes title to the resources contributed by each participant as well as the products or profits.[39] Joint ventures can be contractual or of the equity type. A contractual joint venture will normally be used where the duration or the scope of the activity is limited, or where the laws of the country where the activities are to be conducted do not permit foreign ownership. Technology is usually assigned to the joint venture through a licensing agreement. All the restrictions that we have seen in the licensing context also apply to this situation.

Other arrangements that are used for the transfer of technology include (a) countertrade, a type of agreement in which the supplier of services or technology is required to accept goods or services from their recipient in exchange of the technology and the goods or services it provides; (b) production contracting, a form of industrial cooperation where one party produces goods and services for another in accordance with the specifications, and know-how supplied by that other; (c) product specialization, another form of industrial cooperation where the recipient of the technology is required to limit its production to a narrow range of goods for the technology transferor who then offers a wide range of products to the market; (d) intraenterprise transfers, a device by which a company sets up a wholly owned subsidiary in a foreign country and then transfers the technology to it, an advantageous arrangement because it gives the parent company greater control than it would have without full ownership; and (e) marketing arrangements such as distributorships and franchises. In a distributorship arrangement, a manufacturer supplies goods or services to an entity, which then supplies them to the end users. The manufacturer in this type of arrangement may have to pass along the technology or know-how for the products or services involved. Franchises usually involve a party (franchisee) manufacturing goods utilizing industrial property rights such as a trademark belonging to a franchisor.[40]

At least until recently, NASA policy in cooperative projects has been to transfer as little technology as possible. That policy was best stated by its former Director of International Affairs:

> In projects where there is foreign involvement, that involvement is structured so as to avoid technology transfer. Generally, foreign participants undertake to provide a discrete piece of the overall project and are then responsible for developing the resulting technology and hardware. Only the minimum amount of technical information necessary to ensure effective interface among the various elements of a project is exchanged.[41]

The most typical expression of that policy is the one followed in Spacelab.[42] Article XIII of the NASA-ESRO Spacelab Memorandum of Understanding provides that each of the parties is to retain all rights to patents and/or proprietary information both antedating and postdating the agreement. This concept is amplified in the Spacelab Inter-Governmental Agreement, which provides that the European partners and the United States will have reciprocal access to each others' technology, including "know-how which is needed in order to accomplish successfully their tasks under the cooperative program."[43] Other provisions restrict the European partners, their nationals, and ESRO from making such technology available "beyond" them without express approval by the United States. Furthermore, such access to technology was to be effected in such a way as not to infringe any existing proprietary rights of any person or entity in the United States or Europe.[44] This type of arrangement was largely repeated in the Memoranda of Understanding for phase B of the U.S./International Space Station, which states, inter alia, that the intent of the Parties is to exchange technical information, data, and goods "necessary for the purpose of carrying out the objectives and activities of this cooperative programme."[45] Where, however, the originating party or its contractors believes that such a transfer involves proprietary information, "the parties agree to consult promptly and provide in a timely manner for appropriate protective conditions for its exchange and use within the cooperative program."[46] These two procedures were combined in a draft that in effect creates a policy of efficient exchange among partners of technology and goods that are necessary to fulfill their respective responsibilities.[47]

Export Controls

The purpose of export controls, both national and international, is to deny actual and potential enemies of the West access to Western technologies likely to increase their military threat.[48] These restrictions obviously affect the aerospace industry and the international flow of technology. At the U.S. level, the main statute governing the subject is the *Arms Export Control Act* (AECA).[49] This act authorizes the president to control the export and import of defense articles and defense services "in furtherance of world peace and the security and foreign policy of the United States."[50] The authority was delegated to the secretary of state and is executed by the director of the Office of Munitions Control (OMC) of the Bureau of Politico-Military Affairs within the Department of State.[51] The OMC administers the U.S. Munitions List, which catalogues a number of sensitive articles and services, pursuant to the *International Traffic in Arms Regulation* ITAR.[52] There are a number of categories included in this list. Category IV includes rockets and other launch vehicles, Category XI military and space electronics. Category VIII lists "spacecraft, including manned and unmanned, active and passive satellites." Those items can only be exported with an export license. In order to obtain a license, the applicant must state the country of ultimate destination along with the specific "end user" and "end use" of the articles being exported.[53] If the export is approved, the exporter must incorporate the following statement in the export declaration, bill of lading and invoice:

> These commodities are authorized by the U.S. Government for export only to. . . . They may not be resold, diverted, transferred, transhipped, or otherwise disposed of in any other country, either in their original form or after being incorporated through an intermediate process into other end-items, without the prior written approval of the US Department of State.[54]

The other U.S. statute governing export controls is the *Export Administration Act*, as amended.[55] The Office of Export Administration (OEA) within the Department of Commerce administers the Commodity Control List.[56] In addition to classifying commodities, the list also classifies countries on the basis of their strategic interests versus those of the United States. The two classifications thus provide a cross-reference of which items should not be exported to which countries. The act defines the purpose of the Commodities Control List as follows:

a. to restrict the export of goods and technology that would make a significant contribution to the military potential of any other country or combination of countries that would prove detrimental to the national security of the United States;

b. to restrict the export of goods and technology where necessary to further significantly the foreign policy of the United States or to fulfill its declared international obligations; and

c. to restrict the export of goods where necessary to protect the domestic economy from the excessive drain of scarce materials and to reduce the serious inflationary impact of foreign demand.[57]

Among the items controlled by the act are lasers and robots, including end effectors such as those that were planned to be used with the Mobile Servicing Center of the Space Station. A significant subpart of the Commodities Control List is the Militarily Critical Technologies List, which is maintained under the primary responsibility of the secretary of defense.

On an international level, export controls by Western nations are mostly governed by the *COCOM Procedures* (Coordinating Committee on Multilateral Export Controls). Representatives from COCOM countries (Belgium, Denmark, France, Germany, Greece, Italy, Japan, Luxembourg, The Netherlands, Norway, Portugal, Turkey, and the United Kingdom) meet in Paris where a consultative group and two subordinate committees administer three COCOM lists: a munitions list; an atomic energy list, and an industrial commercial list.[58] In addition to these lists, member countries also maintain their own national lists, which can be quite restrictive.

The logic of export control demands that all sources of technology in the West be controlled in a uniform fashion because restricting technology from a single country is pointless if the same technology is available somewhere else. Thus COCOM is supposed to be a uniform system with which all the Western allies are in agreement. In reality, however, because implementation of the COCOM guidelines is left to individual members, each interprets and executes them differently.[59] The basic difference between COCOM controls and U.S. export controls is that the American ones are more comprehensive, more likely to be vigorously enforced, and involve more severe penalties for infringement. Although there is substantial coordination between the two systems, it can happen that COCOM guidelines will permit a particular technology to be exported, whereas U.S. law will not. This may put the United States in the position of watching foreign companies exporting what American firms may not.

Looking now more specifically at the effects of this regime of export controls on the aerospace industry, the following observations can be made.

As we have seen in the previous chapters, the federal government requires domestic launchers to obtain a launch license for domestic launches licensed under the *Commercial Space Launch Act.* Export licenses, however, are no longer required. Export controls affect instead the export of satellites for launch elsewhere which, in many cases, has been prevented. Commercial communications satellites are specifically excluded from the coverage of the AECA and their export from the United States is therefore only governed by the *Export Administration Act.* Under the act, export cannot be prohibited on security or foreign policy grounds if those items are readily available outside the United States.[60] Also, the provision that safeguards national resources in short supply currently includes strategic resources. In the list provided by the act, items are classified according to technical designations. Satellites are not specifically enumerated in the Commodities Control List, but their components could easily fall into several of the technical categories contained therein, so that the applicability of the act to a specific satellite would depend on its components.[61] A new rule that came into effect September 10, 1993, removes all communications spacecraft parts from the Munitions List.

In the last few years, there has been a trend to reduce the scope of export controls or, at least, to focus on the control of those items that pose a real threat to the United States and its allies. With the collapse of the Soviet Union, the entire outlook on strategic goals and national security has changed and it is still evolving in ways that are difficult to predict.

In a recent interview,[62] Henry Sokolsky, a former deputy for nonproliferation policy at the Pentagon, maintained that distinguishing between technology for space launch vehicles and ballistic missiles is virtually impossible. In his words: "The difference between that Atlas booster that propelled John Glenn into outer space and the Atlas boosters that we used to threaten Russia with nuclear annihilation comes down to one word: attitude. It does not take very long to change the attitude of a missile from 90 degrees for space launch to 45 degrees for a military launch. In addition, countries change their minds and their leadership." He adds, "if the United States sells launch services, that is a fine and decent thing and frankly very close to what we do now. If it exports launch vehicle capability, that is something I oppose. A space launch vehicle is to a missile what a peaceful nuclear explosive device is to a bomb: very, very similar and too close for comfort."

These arguments, no doubt, have validity and yet some disagree because, as noted earlier, export controls can be meaningless if the technology can be acquired somewhere else, as may be the case for launch capability. There has recently been a marked difference between the White House and Congress on the issue of export regulations governing launch technology. A presidential review directive, which includes input from the State, Defense, and Commerce Departments, could be signed by the president in the near future. If the president approves the directive, countries that have agreed to abide by international standards of nonproliferation would be granted greater access to the U.S. space launch technology.[63] The administration is hoping that the relaxation of restrictions on exports of U.S. rocket technology will induce more nations to sign the *1987 Missile Technology Control Regime* (MTCR), which to date has 23 signatories. Several members of Congress are opposing the initiative, arguing that loosening the restrictions would hamper U.S. efforts to curb the spread of ballistic missiles around the globe.

NOTES

1. Scott Sacknoff, unpublished article, July 28, 1993.

2. Andrew Young, *Law and Policy in the Space Station's Era*, Martinus Nijhoff Publishers, Dordrecht, 1989, p. 180.

3. Pub. L. 96–480, October 21, 1980, 94 Stat. 2311 (Title 15 §§ 3701–3714), revised several times until Pub. L. 102–484, Division C, Title XXXI, Subtitle C, § 3135(a), October 23, 1992, 106 Stat 2640 (Title 15 § 3710).

4. Pub. L. 97–219, July 22, 1982, 96 Stat. 217 (Title 15 § 631), revised to October 28, 1992, Title 15 § 638.

5. U.S.C. Title 15 § 4301, extended in 1991.

6. Pub. L. 99–661, November 14, 1986, 100 Stat. 3816.

7. Enacted by the president in April, 1987.

8. Pub. L. 100–418, August 23, 1988, 102 Stat. 1107; Pub. L. 100–570, Title II § 206, October 31, 1988, 102 Stat. 2878 (Title 42 § 62) revised to Pub. L. 102–245, Title I §§ 103(e), 105(d)(f), February 14, 1992, 106 Stat. 9, Title 15 §§ 278/note 1, 4603, 4603(a), and 4632.

9. For a list of the above statutes, see *Technology Applications Program*, Office of Technology Applications, Strategic Defense Initiative Organization, The Pentagon, August 1991.

10. Pub. L. 99–502, October 20, 1986, 100 Stat. 1785 (Title 15 § 3701 *et seq.*; Title 35 § 210.); Pub. L. 101–189 Div. C., Part C, November 29, 1989, 103 Stat. 1674 (Title 15 §§ 3701, 3710, 3719[a] and [c]).

11. At 15 U.S.C. § 3704.

12. 15 U.S.C. § 3705.

13. 15 U.S.C. § 3710(b) and (c).

14. *Ibid.* (d).

15. *Integrating Commercial and Military Technologies for National Strength: an Agenda for Change*, 1991 Report of the Center for Strategic and International Studies Steering Committee on Security and Technology.

16. For a discussion of this topic, see *Spinning Off New Technologies* in Technology Transfer, a supplement to the February 20, 1992, issue of Washington Technology, pp. 5–11.

17. *Ibid.*, at 6.

18. *Id.*

19. *Ibid.*, at 8.

20. See Aerospace Spinoffs, a publication of the NASA Technology Utilization Division, Office of Commercial Programs. No date provided.

21. *Id.*

22. See undated pamphlet by the Office of Commercial Programs, Technology Transfer Division, Code CU, National Aeronautics and Space Administration.

23. *Id.*

24. SDI High Technology Update, Update of the Technology Applications Office of the Ballistic Missile Defense Organization, vol. 3, No. 1, Summer 1993.

25. For a full discussion on the activities of WIPO, see Michael Blakeney, *Legal Aspects of the Transfer of Technology to Developing Countries*, ESC Publishing Limited, Oxford, 1989.

26. *Id.*, at 25.

27. General Assembly Res. 1995(XIX) of 1964.

28. UNCTAD, *Handbook on the Acquisition of Technology by Developing Countries*, 1978, in Blakeney, *supra*, at 24.

29. UN Sales No. E. 73 II. B. 1 (April 1973); Guidelines for the Evaluation of Transfer of Technology Agreements, Development and Transfer of Technology Series, No. 123, 1979.

30. Gouri, *UNIDO View of Technology Use*, Goldscheider and Arnold, 1986, 2F-13, in Blakeney, *supra*, at 26–27.

31. See Blakeney, *supra*.

32. For a full list and discussion, *see* Blakeney, *supra*, at 5–14.

33. WIPO, Model Law for Developing Countries on Inventions, sec. 501, vol. II, 1980, p. 57.

34. See Blakeney, *supra*, at 28.

35. *Id.*

36. See Okono, *Selecting and Adapting Technology*, Finnegan and Goldscheider, *The Law and Business of Licensing*, 1980, 505.243, in Blakeney, *supra* at 34.

37. See Blakeney, *supra*, at 35–42.

38. *Id.*, at 44.

39. *Id.*, at 45.

40. *Id.*, at 46–47.

41. K. S. Pedersen, *International Cooperation and Competition in Space: A Current Perspective*, 11 Journal of Space Law 1983, pp. 21, 23.

42. For cooperative projects in general, see Young, *supra*, pp. 180–182.

43. *Ibid.*, at 181.

44. *Id.*

45. MOU article 9.1.

46. *Ibid.*, article 9.2.

47. Young, *supra*, at 182.

48. Stuart Macdonald, *Technology and the Tyranny of Export Controls*, The Macmillan Press Ltd., London, 1990, p. 9.

49. 22 U.S.C. §§ 2751–2796 (1988).

50. *Ibid.* 22 U.S.C. § 2778(a)(1).

51. See Young, *supra*, at 183.

52. 22 CFR Subchapter M, parts 120–129 (1986).

53. Young, *supra*, at 185.

54. *Id.*

55. Pub. L. 96–72 of September 29, 1979, 93 Stat. 503, as amended by the Export Administration Act of 1985, Pub. L. 99–64, 95 Stat. 1727.

56. 15 CFR, Part 399.

57. 50 U.S.C. § 2402(2).

58. Young, *supra*, at 187.

59. Macdonald, *supra*, at 9.

60. See Timothy A. Brooks, "Negotiating International Trade Law in Launch Series," 6 *High Technology Law Journal*, 1991.

61. *Id.*

62. Space News, August 23, 1993, p. 22.

63. Space News article, August 16, 1993, p. 1.

Selected Bibliography

Benko, Marietta. *Space Law in the United Nations*. Norwell, MAL Kluwer Academic Publishers, 1985.

Blackney, Michael. *Legal Aspects of the Transfer of Technology to Developing Countries*. Oxford: ESC Publishing Limited, 1989.

Christol, Carl Quimby. *Space Law: Past, Present, and Future*. Boston: Kluwer Law and Taxation Publishers, 1991.

d'Angelo, George V. *Aerospace Agencies and Organizations: A Guide for Business and Government*. Westport, CT: Quorum Books, 1993.

Diederiks-Verschoor, Isabella Henrietta Philepina. *An Introduction to Space Law*. Boston: Kluwer Law and Taxation Publishers, 1993.

Finch, Edward Ridley, Jr., and Amanda Lee Moore. *Astrobusiness: A Guide to the Commerce and Law of Outer Space*. New York: Praeger Publishers, 1985.

Goldman, Nathan. *American Space Law: International and Domestic*. Ames, IA: Iowa State University Press, 1988.

______. *Space Policy: An Introduction*. Ames, IA: Iowa State University Press, 1992.

Goodrich, Jonathan. *The Communication of Outer Space: Opportunities and Obstacles for American Business*. Westport, CT: Quorum Books, 1993.

Gorove, Stephen. *Developments in Space Law: Issues and Policies*. Norwell, MA: Kluwer Academic Publishers, 1991.

Meredith, Pamela L. *Space Law: A Case Study for the Practitioner: Implementing a Telecommunications Satellite Business Concept*. Norwell, MA: Kluwer Academic Publishers, 1992.

Okolie, Charles Chukwuma. *International Law of Satellite Remote Sensing and Outer Space*. Dubuque, IA: Kendall/Hunt Publishing Co., 1989.

Reynolds, Glenn H. *Outer Space: Problems of Law and Policy*. Boulder, CO: Westview Press, 1989.

Van Bogaert, E.R.C. *Aspects of Space Law*. Boston: Kluwer Law and Taxation Publishers, 1986.

White, Rita Lauria. *The Law and Regulation of International Space Communication*. Norwood, MA: Artech, 1988.

Young, Andrew J. *Law and Policy in the Space Stations' Era*. Norwell, MA: Kluwer Academic Publishers, 1989.

Index

About the Author

GEORGE V. d'ANGELO is an attorney in private practice. For several years he worked for the Office of Legal Affairs of the United Nations where he was Assistant Secretary to the Legal Subcommittee of the Committee on the Peaceful Uses of Outer Space. He specializes in international law, high technology and aerospace, with particular regard to financing, procurement, joint ventures and acquisitions. Among other works, he is the author of *Aerospace Agencies and Organizations: A Guide to Business and Government* (Quorum, 1993).